Sacrament

A thought for each day of the year

Philip M. Hudson

Copyright 2019 by Philip M. Hudson.

Published 2019.

Printed in the United States of America.

All rights reserved.

No portion of this book may be reproduced, stored in a retrieval system, or transmitted in any form or by any means – electronic, mechanical, photocopy, recording, scanning, or other – except for brief quotations in critical reviews or articles, without the prior written permission of the author.

ISBN 978-1-950647-25-5

Illustrations – Google Images.

This book may be ordered from online bookstores.

Publishing Services by BookCrafters
Parker, Colorado.
www.bookcrafters.net

Table of Contents

Acknowledgements..1
Preface..3
Introduction...5
365 Minute Musings..7

About The Author...373
By The Author..375
What More Can I Say?..379

Every
time we worthily
partake of the bread and
water of the Sacrament, we are
powerfully strengthened, so that the
promises of heaven might be realized.
We invite virtue to garnish our thoughts
unceasingly. As our confidence builds,
the doctrine of the priesthood distils
upon our heads as the dews from
heaven, the Holy Ghost is our
constant companion, and its
guidance flows unto us
without compulsion.

Acknowledgements

In this volume, I have attributed quotations to original authors whenever possible, as well as when I have editorialized their ideas. In many cases, however, my language will naturally reflect the teachings of leaders and members of The Church of Jesus Christ of Latter-day Saints.

The list of those who have contributed to this book is endless. As I have organized my own thoughts, I have realized how heavily I have borrowed from the towering examples of those who, over the years, have been my mystical mentors, my sensible chaperones, my spiritual guides, my surrogate saviors, my compassionate critics, and everything in between.

They are my avatars, manifestations of deity in bodily forms, my na'vi, the visionaries, who communicate with God on a level to which I can only aspire, and my tsaddik, whom I esteem as intuitive interpreters of biblical law and scripture. They are my divine teachers incarnate. They have offered listening ears, extended open arms, lifted my spirits, shown me the way, stretched my mind, reinforced my faith, strengthened my testimony, helped me to discover my wings, given immaterial support, provided of their means, emboldened me with words of encouragement, cheered me on with wise counsel, taught me humility, been there to steady me, soothed my troubled soul, stepped in to nurture me, led me to fountains of living water, wet my parched lips with inspired counsel, and bound up my wounds.

When I think of the influence of a multitude of angels thinly disguised as my family, friends, and peers, I remember the words of Sir Isaac Newton, who, when pressed to reveal the great secret behind his accomplishments, simply replied: "I stood on the shoulders of giants." Of course, at the end of the day, I alone am responsible for the content of this volume. But I hope my interpretations of principles and doctrine will cultivate your interest to dig deeper into the themes woven into this tapestry, by turning to the scriptures and seeking inspiration from the Spirit. My only goal is to help you to expand your insights into the telestial mile markers, the terrestrial truths, and the celestial guidelines that accompany each of us during our quest for enlightenment through the Sacrament.

Preface

I love to learn by reading the scriptures, and I often think of St. Hilary, who wrote in the third century: "Scripture consists not in what we read, but in what we understand." In each of the musings within this volume, I have consistently tried to find a scriptural foundation and a spiritual confirmation as I put my pen to paper.

I am continually reminded of Nephi's counsel to press forward with complete dedication and steadfastness, or confidence with a firm determination in Christ, having a perfect brightness of hope, or perfect faith, and charity, or a love of God and of all men. If we do this, feasting upon the word of Christ, or receiving strength and nourishment as we ponder the doctrines of the kingdom, and particularly that of the Sacrament, and as we then endure to the end in righteousness, we shall have eternal life, which is the greatest of God's gifts. (See 2 Nephi 31:20).

It is with love, then, that I extend to you the invitation to enjoy this omnibus of random thoughts. Embrace it at face value, and use its observations relating to the Sacrament as a springboard to your own personal plateaus of discovery, as you are taught by the Spirit to move in the direction of your dreams.

It
is in the
Sacrament
that our hearts
are knit together in
unity and in love. It is
an important experience
that gives those who are
living on both sides of
the veil the tools they
need to confront
eternity.

Introduction

If they are fortunate, novice quilters quickly learn a bit of wisdom from the Amish, who make some of the finest quilts in the world. On purpose, the Amish build mistakes into their projects, because they believe that any attempt on their part to design and produce a flawless creation would be a mockery of God, Who alone is perfect. The humility of the Amish makes me think of my own weak attempts to put the thoughts expressed in this omnibus to paper. In His infinite wisdom, God knows very well that I do not need to consciously plan on lacing my efforts with errors. That will come quite naturally, without the need for me to intentionally contribute to my short-comings.

Perhaps this serendipitous collection of musings will do little more than help to define quirks in my personality. Each of us is different, and many things, including our family and friends, the circumstances in which we find ourselves, the quality of our education, and our own personalities, inspire and mold our oral and written expressions. I would like to think that, in this text, all of these influences have been encouraging, affirmative, and constructive.

The reflections within this tome leave the door ajar for the reader, to allow shafts of the light of understanding to creep in. If, as I have expressed my thoughts, I mis-stated myself a few times, or flat-out got it wrong, I ask the patient indulgence and gentle correction of the reader.

Too often, I realize that my communications can be "carefully disguised with hypocrisy and glittering words," as Einstein put it. Although I do fancy myself a wordsmith, I have tried to avoid pedestrian expressions, idle language, and lazy scholarship. I do not pretend to be an authority on the doctrine of the Sacrament, inasmuch as I believe that we are all works in progress, but if you find the factual tone of a particular musing disengaging, the truth is that I typically experienced a deep personal involvement in my interpretation of the principles that illuminated its meaning.

In any event, when you open this volume, I hope you ponder these minute musings with as much enjoyment as I have experienced while creating them.

As we endure to
the end in righteousness,
the Sacrament, which is, at first
blush, a covenant of sanctification,
guides us toward our eternal destiny in
the Kingdom of God. It is after we have
partaken of the emblems of Christ that
the Spirit qualifies us for the blessings
that are related to the covenants of
both justification and exaltation.
The road to the Sacrament
table continues on, to
the House of the
Lord.

It is in this
life that we prepare for
a reunion with our Heavenly
Father, as we strive to become
holy before Him. Our participation
in the Sacrament as we seek the Spirit
is the tangible expression of our plea
to the Savior to come to our rescue,
and in particular to rely upon His
Atonement to heal the damage
that has been inflicted by sin
in consequence of the
weaknesses in our
armor.

Meet Joe Black is
a film that was loosely
based on the 1934 production
entitled "Death Takes a Holiday."
In the final scene, the protagonist,
who is about to die, asks Death: "Should
I be afraid?" When Death answers him and
says: "Not a man like you, Bill," we know that,
in the face of the inevitable, everything is going
to be all right. May we never find ourselves more
than a week away from the last time we have
partaken of the Sacrament, so that when it
is our turn for heaven to wrap us in its
warm embrace, we will be blessed
with a similar reassurance.

Every Sabbath, the Spirit testifies we are children of God. Of this truth, there is no question. We know this intuitively, for "the Spirit itself beareth witness with our spirit." (Romans 8:16). This is one of the reasons we so enjoy our Sacrament service.

We partake
of the Sacrament in
a process of generation,
and not just of maturation.
Mortality has been designed to
be a lifelong learning laboratory
to give each of us the opportunity to
mold our nature so that it more closely
resembles that of God. He initiated the
Sacrament that we might experience a
spiritual transformation. We would
undergo a metamorphosis but we
would emerge from the chrysalis
of our covenant relationship
with God as eagles, and
not as butterflies.

In
the Sacrament,
all of our trappings
and pretenses are shorn
away, as outward observances
and phylacteries are stripped from
the ritual of our worship, until only
our true feelings remain. We bear
our souls before God, angels,
and witnesses.

Our faith notwithstanding, we are saved by the grace of God, after all we can do, and that is primarily to repent, be baptized, and to be renewed by the Sacrament.

Temporal baggage
can create an imbalance in
our lives that leads to confusion.
The Sacrament can jar us out of our
collective complacency by upsetting the
stagnation of the status quo. It invites us
to enjoy a settled conviction in our minds
by getting our juices flowing, prodding us
to constructively expend our energy, and
putting our agency to work. It compels
us to be doers, to be actively engaged,
and more than simply hearers. Those
who partake of the Sacrament make
things happen, while timid souls
whose tentative steps cannot
quite propel them all the
way to the emblems of
Christ are doomed to
ask what happened.

When we have been
privileged to reach out
and touch the face of God,
as we do during our Sacrament
services, the Spirit that is present can
be augmented by the medium of music.
Even before the foundations of the earth
were laid, a celestial harmony floated
in the air, when "the morning stars
sang together, and all the sons
of God shouted for joy."
(Job 38:7).

In moments of deep reflection, as before the Sacrament table, we envision "stepping on shore, and finding it heaven! We visualize taking hold of a hand, and finding it God's hand. We dream of passing from storm and tempest to an unbroken calm, and of waking up, and finding it home." (Anonymous).

Perhaps it is because it is so easy to get out of focus, lose our grip on the iron rod, and wander from strict obedience to the neglect of our covenants, that we are commanded to regularly and repetitively participate in the ordinance of the Sacrament. As we do so each week, it is not vain repetition. We think of it as theatrical encore.

We partake
of the Sacrament
that we might learn to
abide by the laws of heaven,
even as we tarry upon the earth.
We yearn for our hearts to burn
within us, and for the Spirit to
speak to us, so that it might
open up the scriptures to
our understanding.

The invitation to forgive and to be forgiven is juxtaposed against the sense of despair, despondency, misery, and desperation that is often a part of our mortal schooling when we choose to ignore the blessing of the Sacrament.

The fulcrum of the Sacrament is the doctrine of the Atonement, and the principles of repentance, baptism, and forgiveness. These just happen to be the polar opposites of life without light.

When
we partake of
Sacrament, we enjoy
feelings of harmony and
serenity, in ways that have
been thoughtfully designed
by our Heavenly Father to
touch our heart strings.
These inner stirrings
defy any rational
explanation.

The
Sacrament
blesses us to be
able to reach out
and touch the face of
God with an incorruptible
and unimpeachable spiritual
sixth sense that finds its
expression deep inside
us, within our own
hearts.

We know by the
casualty count from the
ideological War in Heaven, that
some of Heavenly Father's children
have forfeit their privilege to obtain a
body. For those who remained faithful in
the pre-earth existence, however, there have
come humbling liabilities, and so The Plan
required our Heavenly Father to create the
ordinance of the Sacrament, that we might
all have the means to regularly recalibrate
our sights on the glory of our former
home in heaven. The Sacrament thus
becomes a beacon of light in a
lone and dreary world.

The Sacrament speaks to our spirits, for every Gospel principle carries within itself a witness that it is true. Its language is universal, and when the Spirit illuminates our minds, we enjoy a fluency and a familiarity that puts us at ease with principles and doctrine. We are comfortable with the revealed word of God and look forward to vistas of eternal proportion that open up before our eyes.

Wordsworth wrote: "Heaven lies about us in our infancy. Shades of the prison house begin to close upon the growing boy. But he beholds the light and whence it flows; he sees it in his joy. The youth, who daily farther from the east must travel, still is nature's priest. And by the vision splendid, is on his way attended. At length, the man perceives it die away, and fade into the light of common day." This is why we need to partake of the Sacrament.

We
feel that we
are as lights that
are set on a hill, when
we partake of the Sacrament.
We build up our discipleship with
dignity, and we make it honorable. We
enlarge and strengthen our callings, and
we simply perform the service that pertains
to them. We are like a pair of old shoes,
to be worn out in service.

The living water that spiritually sustains us is the doctrine of the Gospel of Jesus Christ, including the covenant we make with God at the waters of baptism. Later, we symbolically renew that covenant in the ordinance of the Sacrament.

The emblems of Christ are little packets of light that contribute just the right amount of illumination that is critically needed by a world that has become enveloped in thick darkness.

If we step
away from the
world of confusion
to take up our cross,
follow the difficult path
to our own Gethsemane, and
partake of the Sacrament, we very
quickly recognize that our Heavenly
Father has created the well-established
pattern that leads to our Christ-centered
life. The ordinance allows us to regularly
recommit ourselves to internalize every
truth relating to eternal progression,
and endows us with the power to
endure every adversity, that we
might see life through to its
pre-ordained end, and do
so in righteousness.

We partake
of the Sacrament
that we might come
in the unity of the faith,
and of the knowledge of the
Son of God unto the stature of
the fulness of Christ. As we make
that journey, we retain our distinct
individuality as the spirt born sons
and daughters of God, but we are
unified in every other way.

There is
an ever-present
negative energy that
influences our affairs,
and the Sacrament is a
useful countermeasure.
Its sole stipulations are
that we confess when we
have, in any magnitude,
embraced the opposites
that lie before us, and
that we immediately
undertake the safety
protocols required
by repentance to
bring us back to
harmony with
our home in
heaven.

An early leader of the Reformation, Roger Williams, declared: "There is no regularly constituted church on earth, nor any person authorized to administer any church ordinance, nor can there be until new apostles are sent by the Great Head of the Church, for Whose Coming I am seeking." Thank be to God for the restoration of the Gospel, and for those who answered the faithful petitions of those who for so long had sought the one true church that had the authority to bless the lives of the people with the ordinances to which Williams referred.

It might
come as a pleasant
surprise to discover that
when we have been spiritually
begotten of Jesus Christ, we are
given the invitation to re-write the
record of our lives. We cannot go
back and start a new beginning,
but we can begin now to make
a new ending. Our lives can
become fairytales that are
waiting to be written by
the omnipotent finger
of God.

When we partake of the Sacrament, we are blessed with the courage to be "witnesses of God at at all times and in all things, and in all places." (Mosiah 18:9). We join with a chorus of voices that testifies of His might, majesty, power, and dominion. We dare not shirk our responsibility, for we are under covenant to do so.

We partake
of the Sacrament
that we might reconnect
with our spiritual Birth Parents,
for we are the sons and daughters
of "the living God." (Hosea 1:10). "The
Spirit itself beareth witness with our spirit,
that we are the children of God." (Romans
8:16). We find answers to our yearning to
know: "Have we not all one father?" We
are inspired to ask the question: "Hath
not one God created us?"
(Malachi 2:10).

In the
Sacrament, we
enjoy a familiarity
with principles that is in
sharp contrast to society's
tenets that are continually
morphed by the shifting sands
of cultural expediency. Each week,
we renew the sacramental covenant to
protect us from the constantly mutating
values of the world. On our own, we could
never keep up with its current definition
of morality, because its flavor of the day
is always changing. In contrast, God's
undeviating standard of behavior
defines an unchanging moral
base that shapes us as we
mature into the full
stature of our
spirits.

When we
turn our backs
on the invitation to
sup with our Heavenly
Father thru the Sacrament,
and if we remain alienated
from Him by spiritual death, it
is unavoidable that we must
eventually surrender to
inclinations that are
carnal, sensual,
and devilish.

The Sacrament can catalyze our relationship with God, when it unshackles us from the icy grip of our captivity to Satan; and all is due to the Atonement of Christ.

When we are assaulted from all
sides by sounding brass and tinkling
cymbals, those with a strong testimony of the
efficacy of the Sacrament will find within
themselves the ability to sift through the
discordant cacophony of confusing
voices to find revealed truth,
as they are touched
by the Spirit.

It is the
Sacrament that
helps us to redefine
and redesign what had
heretofore been stumbling
blocks. They are repurposed
into the very stepping stones
that are needed to conquer
our fears, reinvigorate our
confidence, and overcome
the obstacles that are
strewn about along
the path of our
progression.

Moses counseled the Israelites to build upon the Rock of their salvation. He urged them to "write (their covenants) upon the posts of (their) houses" and to "not appear before the Lord empty" handed. (Deuteronomy 6:9 & 16:16). We would do well to do likewise, by remembering our covenant of the Sacrament, as we take His name upon ourselves, and promise to keep his commandments and always remember Him, that we might always have His Spirit to be with us.

"For behold, it is as easy to give heed to the word of Christ, which will point to you a straight course to eternal bliss, as it was for our fathers to give heed to this compass, which would point unto them a straight course to the promised land." (Alma 37: 44). So it is with us. Christ is our ablest Navigator, and when we follow the course that He has charted that leads us to Sacrament meeting, we will find that no wind can blow except it fills our sails.

The Sacrament establishes a relationship with the Holy Ghost that invites Him to stand right beside us, and to weigh in on one side of the scale even as the counterfeit coin of Satan's spurious currency clatters down in a cacophony of confusion on the other side of the scale.

Every single time
a child of God partakes
of the Sacrament, the advancing
tide of wickedness slows just a bit,
and the future looks sunnier. A
thousand points of light, when
gathered as one in Sacrament
meeting, cast a very long
shadow, and hold out
the promise of a
brighter day.

To
paraphrase
the Apostle Paul:
Thanks be to God that
the Sacrament has given
us the opportunity to lead
quiet and peaceful lives
in all godliness and
in all honesty.

We have a
lot to learn, and hopefully,
we have the gift of time on our
side. If we do, perhaps we should think
about what we would like to discover in the
next twelve months. How would we like to be
different then, from what we are now? How can
partaking of the Sacrament roughly 48 times
in the coming year help us to make positive
changes in our lives? As we consider that
challenge, we recall the familiar adage:
Some men see things as they are, and
ask why? Others dream things that
never were, and ask why not?
Give me one good reason
why you should not let
the Spirit guide you
as never before.

Our life
long learning
laboratory within
which we find ourselves
gives every one of God's
children the opportunity to
mold themselves so they might
more closely resemble His nature.
He initiated the Sacrament to make
that difficult transformation easier
for us to experience.

It is for
our benefit
that we become
acquainted with evil
as well as with good, with
pain as well as with pleasure,
with darkness as well as with light,
with error as well as with truth, and
with punishment for the infraction of
God's eternal laws, as well as with the
blessings that follow our obedience. The
Sacrament is designed to be our ace in
the hole, that thru the Atonement, we
might remember our covenant of
baptism no matter where on the
journey of life we might find
ourselves, or in what state
of affairs we might
currently be in.

If we
want to
harness the
power of the
Sacrament, we
must be humble
and gentle, and be
easily entreated; be
tolerant, patient, and
long-suffering, and be
temperate in all things.
We must take care to keep
the commandments, and ask
for whatsoever temporal and
spiritual blessings we stand in
need of, always giving thanks
for what we have received. We
nurture our faith, our hope,
and our charity, and make
every effort to abound
in good works.

It is because of the
Sacrament, that, as fire in
the sky, the air in the theater of
life is charged with an electricity that
represents the inevitable merger of the
universal encouragement of the Light of
Christ with the guidance provided by the Holy
Ghost. Streaking in tandem across the heavens,
their trajectories coalesce to trace a flaming
trail that sparkles over a vast cosmic ocean
that is alive with energy. Over the ebb and
flow of its tide, God creates a bridge of
understanding between the secular and
the divine, that is buttressed by the
cohesive influence of the mighty
foundation of our faith.

It is the fortification of the Sacrament that protects us from the snares of Satan, that exist to steal from us that which is most precious: even our spiritual identity as children of God.

We partake
of the Sacrament
because we want to
be redeemed of God;
to be numbered among
those who will participate
in the first resurrection,
that we might enjoy
eternal life.

The Sacrament fans our fire of resolve with a faith to hope and pray to have courage to change the things we can, for the serenity to accept the things we cannot, and for the wisdom to know the difference.

We
partake
of the Sacrament,
that we might be given
the tools we need in order
to lengthen our stride. In a
confrontation of principles with
values that may tear at the fabric of
the natural world, the Savior asks us
to exert ourselves with actions that
will surely stretch the limits of our
ability. But in the process, we will
find that there is, in the Holy,
Ghost, an unlimited source
of spiritual strength.

We who
come to the
Sacrament table
are pure in heart.
We enjoy the intrinsic
countermeasures to wicked
imaginations. Our behavior is
driven by altruism, self-denial,
self-discipline, self-restraint,
and self-sacrifice; these all
come as we listen with our
hearts to the promptings
of the Spirit that wash
over us as a gentle
breeze.

The
Sacrament
is nurtured within
the rich culture medium
of faith, validated by baptism
in a metaphysical reunion with
God. It is witnessed in the fiery
cauldron of the Spirit, in the
only way that is possible,
to ransom us from our
sins and keep us
on the strait
path.

Those
of a weak
will, who have
lost their desire to
partake of the Sacrament,
have often simply exchanged
the blessings of heaven and earth
for the provocative pleasures that are
provided by the pandering purveyors of
poor choices. They quickly become snared
by the Devil and are bound by his strong
chains. Too late, they realize that their
misguided loyalty has limited their
options, restricted their actions,
fettered their self-expression,
and shut the door on the
guiding influence of
the Spirit.

The Sacrament speaks to our spirits, for every Gospel principle carries within itself a witness that it is true. Its language is universal, and when the Holy Ghost illuminates our minds, we enjoy fluency, familiarity, and ease with the doctrines, and comfort with the revealed words of God that open up vistas of eternal proportion before our eyes.

"For behold, it is as easy
to give heed to the word of Christ,"
that is expressed in the Sacrament prayer,
"which will point to you a straight course to
eternal bliss, as it was for our fathers to give
heed to this compass, which would point unto
them a straight course to the promised land."
(Alma 37: 44). As it was for Alma and his
people, so it is for us today. Christ is our
Navigator. He is our Liahona. He is the
wind beneath our wings. If we will
follow Him, we will discover that
no wind can blow except
it fills our sails.

When we
are baptized,
and then when
we partake of the
Sacrament, the Plan
itself is initialized. The
ordinances provide us with
an insight into our spiritual
roots that are the products of
our interconnectivity and
our interdependence
with each other
and with
God.

We receive
the Sacrament
that Heavenly Father
might create in our behalf
an impenetrable shield of faith
in our Lord Jesus Christ. Each of
us has been fitted with protection that
has been tailored to our unique and
distinctive needs. Its elements are
defined and fortified by the
covenants we make
with Him.

We are
given an
extra measure
of resolve to see
life thru to its end,
when we partake of the
Sacrament. If challenges
seem overwhelming, the
covenant stands ready
to offer assistance
that is related to
their resolution.

It seems indisputable that the object and design of our existence, following our participation in Sacrament services, would be to become the happiest people upon the face of the earth. Obedience unleashes a spiritual cornucopia. We feast upon the nourishing bread of life that has been provided, and drink copiously from a well of living water. Life could not be better!

As we partake during the ordinance of the Sacrament, we are most pleasantly surprised to discover that the Savior is on our right, and on our left, and in our hearts. We are strengthened by a multitude of angels thinly disguised as our family and friends. We recall the words of Sir Isaac Newton, who, when he was pressed to reveal the secret behind his accomplishments, simply replied: "I stood on the shoulders of giants." The Savior and the Holy Ghost are our giants.

The Sacrament
instills within us a
sound understanding as
we search the scriptures, that
we might know the word of God.
But this is not all; we give ourselves
to prayer, and fasting, that we might
enjoy the spirit of prophecy, and the
spirit of revelation, so that when
we teach, we teach with power
and authority of God.

The Sacrament blesses us with the currency of faith that accrues with interest. We quietly persevere as the disciples of Christ, because we know that the wages of sin is death. The work of the ministry is the only endeavor on earth where the retirement benefits are simply out of this world.

All who
participate in
Sacrament meeting
and are touched by the
Spirit realize that they are
the nobility of heaven, and
that theirs is a divine destiny.
They are counted among those
of a choice and chosen
generation.

During the
administration
of the Sacrament by the
brethren of the priesthood,
our attention is riveted upon
our witness of the Savior, which
the covenant encourages us to
nurture. Every day thereafter,
when we take the temperature
of our testimony, we hope
to be able to detect its
feverish pitch.

Angels will
minister to our needs
because of our participation in
Sacrament meeting. "For I will go
before your face," promised the Lord.
"I will be on your right hand, and
on your left, and my Spirit shall
be in your hearts, and mine
angels round about you,
to bear you up."
(D&C 84:88).

Simply put, the Sacrament exposes us to the process by which we progress. God conceived the ordinance to test our mettle. This is why having the courage be true to our convictions is so intimately tied to righteousness. Only when we act on the basis of faith will we receive a confirmation of the power behind the ordinance, as feelings of self-confidence grow and purposeful action replaces our tentative overtures. The Sacrament releases the potential within us.

When our priorities
are out of order, we lose the
power to bring about positive change.
The Sacrament sharpens our perspective,
enabling us to comprehend and build
upon principles of perfection that
are validated by the Spirit and
emulated by the example of
the Savior Who is the very
centerpiece of the
ordinance.

The Sacrament makes a modest and self-effacing public statement about a profound private conviction.

The Sacrament
invites us to consider
the possibility that we might
one day be like the Savior, for
we believe that His grace consists
of the gifts and power by which we
may be brought to His perfection
and His stature. We believe in a
coming day, He will bless us
not only with what He has,
but also with what
He is.

The
Sacrament coherently
stitches foundation principles
together into an easily recognizable
pattern, so that the power of the word
and the witness of truth may be
conveyed without the need
for external warrant.

Partaking of the Sacrament
is a definitive step on our journey
to Christ. The path that lies beyond the
ordinance leads all the way to the Tree
of Life. It is not a freeway, but a toll
road. Until we have paid the requisite
levy, we cannot hope to comprehend
with fluency the language of the
Spirit that clearly explains what
we must do to make our way
to the tree, that we might
harvest its fruit.

The Sacrament helps us to appreciate how all three members of the Godhead work in our behalf to provide the blessings of immortality and eternal life. In the waters of baptism, we keep the commandment of God; by the Holy Ghost, we will be justified before His throne; and by the redeeming blood of the Savior of the world, we will be sanctified to kneel at His feet before His throne.

During a
week when most
people will not take
the time to stop and smell
the roses, we are reminded by
the Sacrament how reflection can
be uplifting, especially when it is the
Holy Ghost that lights up our features.
As Alma asked the people of Zarahemla:
"Now, behold, I ask of you, my brethren of
the church, have ye spiritually been born
of God? Have ye received His image in
your countenances (and) experienced
this mighty change in your heart?"
(Alma 5:14).

The foundation of the Kingdom of God God is planted on bedrock, as was the wall that was built by an Irishman around his farm. Asked why he made it five feet high and eight feet wide, he replied that if the wind ever blew so hard that it toppled the wall, it would still be five feet wide. There is a redundancy that is built into our covenants, and in their repetition, we are protected by a shield of faith that is, for us, always at least five feet wide.

Joseph Smith taught:
"We may profit by noticing the first intimation of the spirit of revelation; for instance, when we feel pure intelligence flowing into us, it may give us sudden strokes of ideas … By learning the Spirit of God and understanding it, we may grow into the principle of revelation." The Sacrament, then, is a schoolmaster that is designed to bring us, by that same spirit of revelation to the doctrine of our Lord and Savior, Jesus Christ.

Every
time we come to
Church to partake of the
Sacrament, it is as if it were
a contemporary declaration to
the world of tidings of great joy.
It carries us on a groundswell of
emotion that lifts us heavenward.
Worship is elevated to something
more dynamic than the simple
mechanical observance of a
multiplicity of ceremonial
rules. Publishing peace is
the daily antidote to
worldly tendencies
that canker our
souls.

As we
partake of
the Sacrament,
gratitude fills our
hearts as we think of
the infinite Atonement
of the Lord. We examine our
lives through the magnifying
glass of the Spirit to look for
ways to improve. Because of
the Sacrament, we can fly
higher than eagles; the
Savior becomes the
wind beneath our
wings.

The Sacrament
is the spiritual equivalent
to being well-grounded. It is
a powerful positive motivator. We
remember Nephi, who described those
who were "pressing forward, and they came
forth and caught hold of the end of the Rod
of Iron; and they did press forward through
the mist of darkness, clinging to the Rod
of Iron, even until they did come forth
and partake of the fruit of the tree."
(1 Nephi 8:24).

The administration of the Sacrament clears our minds so that we can focus on eternity against the backdrop of the everyday world to which all of us will speedily return.

One of the blessings
of the Sacrament is that it
may inflict upon us a benevolent
blindness that actually helps us to
see more clearly than those with 20:20
vision. Those who worthily partake of the
emblems of Christ feel with a vibrancy
that is incorporeal and indefinable.
It kindles a light within our hearts
that supersedes any and all
of the somatic senses,
and it is far more
valuable.

The ordinance
of the Sacrament must surely
be the prototypical example of the
absolute genius behind God's Plan of
Salvation, as it focuses our minds and
our spirits on our covenants, the Savior,
His Atonement, and on the commandments.
That discipline expands the capacity of
our understanding, and allows us to
experience how a Gospel-centered
life can be greater than the
sum of its parts.

The Sacrament is a scale that measures the strength of our integrity and of our discipleship. It is a barometer that illustrates how spirituality can be inextricably interwoven into our character. The Sacrament beckons us to pattern our lives after the example of the Savior, that we might internalize Gospel principles, and demonstrate obedience to priesthood covenants.

Keeping the covenant we make at the Sacrament table positions us beyond the influence of the adversary and endows us with the power necessary to overcome evil and obtain exaltation. The Prophet Joseph Smith taught that our hope of salvation consists of the Savior placing us beyond the power of our personal enemies. He was referring to those things that hinder our progression, such as greed, dishonesty, immorality, lying, and other vices.

Without
the Sacrament,
our hearts are too
easily set upon the things
of the world. Our spirituality
may be weakened until we no
longer look forward to worship
as our habitual routine. We settle
for an economy hotel room, having
dismissed from our minds the four-star
all-inclusive world class accommodation
that continues to extend its invitation from
just beyond the parted veil of our covenant
of baptism. The only resort fee that we
must pay in order to reclaim its
delights is to have clean hands,
and a pure heart.

From a
Gospel perspective,
our discipline involves the
consistent exercise of agency
as we embrace ennobling eternal
principles with action that is simply
the right thing to do, although it may
not be easy or convenient. If we desire
positive outcomes, free will needs to be
accompanied by the courage to exercise
moral discipline that finds its expression
in our righteous behavior. That leads to
the Sacrament table, but it also just as
powerfully flows from the covenant
of baptism that is renewed in the
ordinance of the Sacrament
on a weekly basis.

Sooner or later,
every member of the Church
evolves into a second-miler. We
do so, not so much by maturation,
but by generation as we are born
of God. We are encouraged to
run, and not just walk, as
we endure to the end
in righteousness.

Living water is
so crucial to our well-being,
that the Lord has provided a conduit
that can penetrate solid limestone, as it
were, so that it may freely flow into our
lives. This conduit is chiseled through
our rough exterior and our stony
nature with the tools of faith,
obedience, study, prayer,
good works, and other
healthy lifestyle
choices.

All of us have been given the Sacrament as the group sharing segment of a work release program that has been revealed by God, to see how we will behave when we are left on our own, after having received unambiguous instruction from above, relating to what we should be doing with the time that we have been allotted during our turn on earth.

The Sacrament
evenly distributes the
weight of our temporal
baggage, that we might
more easily enter in
at the strait and
narrow gate.

The
Sacrament
blesses us with
the tools we need
to calibrate our lives
so that they conform to
the pattern of our heavenly
home. We have come to earth
from the eternal vantage point
of the abode of the Gods. Thus,
Heavenly Father caused that our
celestial chronometer be attuned
to a more easily recognizable
temporal scale. At the same
time, he gave us a hint of
heaven by blessing us
with the Sacrament.

We partake of
emblems of the Sacrament
that we might overcome our
spiritual death by coming into the
presence of our Father and His Son, by
way of the Holy Ghost. His Spirit dazzles
us with an endless reserve of revelation. It
provides illumination to every corner of our
minds and our spirits. The promised blessings
that are proffered by the combined capacity
of the intrinsic light that radiates from all
three members of the Godhead is virtually
beyond description. The binding covenant
that is articulated in the prayer bridges
the gulf between the secular and the
divine that, in other circumstances,
might exist for us. It is no small
coincidence that the names of
the Father, the Son, and the
Holy Ghost are referenced
by name in the words
of the prayer.

The faithfully
penitent submit their
will to the Spirit that,
with their hands raised
to the Most High God,
their incomings, their
outgoings, and their
salutations might
be in the name
of the Lord.

No
wind can
blow except
it fills our sails to
carry each of us ever
closer to our destinations,
without delay or disruption,
and without unnecessary cost,
loss, or detriment. Those with
the desire to participate in the
ordinances of salvation need
only sacrifice their broken
heart and contrite spirit,
which thing is a small
price to pay for
salvation.

"If ye will enter in by the way" and worthily partake of the Sacrament, the Spirit "will show unto you all things what ye should do. Behold, this is the doctrine of Christ."
(2 Nephi 32:5-6).

Standing in opposition to the
grace of God is a darkness that
is so great that it has the potential
to cover the earth, and gross darkness
the people. Without repentance, baptism,
the Atonement, and the Sacrament, we
would become subject to the evil
source of that darkness,
to rise no more.

If God did not make covenants with His children, if there were no law given, if men and women could sin with impunity, "what could justice do, or mercy either, for they would have no claim upon the creature? The works of justice would be destroyed, and God would (simply) cease to be God." (Alma 42:21-22).

In the
Sacrament,
we recognize
that Jesus Christ
is the Son of God,
the Father of heaven
and earth, and is the
Creator of all things.
We honor His name,
and bear it with
respect and
reverence.

As we partake of the Sacrament, we keep ourselves oriented toward the light. However, as our knowledge grows, so do the borders of darkness that encroach upon the edge of the light. The more we know, the more we realize how much we have to learn.

When the law is woven
into the sinews of our souls, so that
it becomes the tapestry of our lives and
is the very pattern upon which we trace our
movement along the path of progression, our
minds will "become single to God, and the
days will come that (we) shall see him,
for he will unveil his face" to us.
(D&C 88:68).

The Sacrament gives our spiritual muscles pliancy and flexibility, that there might be room for the companionship of the Holy Ghost, who makes Himself "manifest unto the children of men, according to their faith" in Jesus Christ. (Jarom 1:4).

We partake
of the Sacrament
so that we might press
forward with steadfastness,
having a perfect brightness of
hope and a love of God and of
our brothers and sisters, feasting
upon the scriptures, as we
endure to the end in
righteousness.

We partake of the
emblems of bread and water
so that we might feel not only
the spiritual intensity, but also the
tangible significance, of the covenant
we are making with our Heavenly Father.
We feel a palpable connection with the
Spirit that washes over us in concentric
waves as its ripple effect influences
everything within our path.

In
the Sacrament,
we consecrate our
lives to the Savior. We
cast ourselves on an altar
of faith whose foundation is
buttressed by a supernal display
of divine direction. We are driven
forward by unwavering confidence
that His power to save might be
unleashed in our behalf and
flow over our wounds as a
healing balm, so that we
might be able to meet
His penetrating gaze
with unencumbered
hearts and clear
eyes.

We receive the Sacrament in a dramatic validation of the influence of the Light of Christ, and of the power of the Holy Ghost. They will labor in tandem among us "till we all come in the unity of the faith, and of the knowledge of the Son of God, unto a perfect man, unto the measure of the stature of the fulness of Christ." (Ephesians 4:13).

In the Sacrament, we experience the excitement of being spiritually begotten of Him, and of having our hearts changed through faith on His name. We turn our thoughts to Him as we feel His energy building within us.

Whether we are
professional athletes
or practiced panhandlers,
living in the fast or the slow
lane of life, whether we have rags
or riches, are leaders or lepers, are
early prodigies or late bloomers, venture
capitalists or welfare recipients; no matter
what our situation may be, the Sacrament
builds a bridge over the troubled waters
of faltering faith. We move beyond the
yellow brick road that leads to Oz, to
the strait and narrow path that will
guide us unerringly to the gates
of heaven itself.

Our participation in the ordinance of the Sacrament helps us to use opposition as the grand key it was intended to be, to open up a portal to the Spirit. In our obedience, we stand independent of all creatures, save our Heavenly Father, Jesus Christ, and the Holy Ghost. When we have completed the journey to the Godhead, that for all intents and purposes began in the Garden, the principle that there is opposition in all things will be indefinitely suspended.

Before the Sacrament table, as before the holy altars in the temple, we make sacred covenants with the Lord, the fulfillment of which will bring us earthly blessings and eternal exaltation. As we focus our attention on obeying His commandments and being worthy to enter the temple and to partake of the Sacrament, our thirst will be quenched with the living water provided by the Gospel of Jesus Christ.

As we participate in the ordinance of the Sacrament, we become more and more like our Father in Heaven. Its repetition nurtures spiritual growth; its reiteration encourages us to faithful obedience, and to more pointedly follow the example of the Savior.

Some people see things as they are, and ask "Why? In the Sacrament, our attention is focused on things that never were, that we might ask "Why not?" It prepares us for a rendezvous with destiny. It carries us above and beyond the shattered dreams of lost souls, to a sanctuary where we may "flourish in immortal youth, unhurt amidst the war of elements, the wreck of matter, and the crash of worlds." (Joseph Addison).

The steadiness of the Sacrament stands as the polar opposite of the moral equivocation, the intellectual instability, the cultural confusion and spiritual schizophrenia that we witness all around us in the world today. We stand in holy places and we are not moved because we we cannot find stable ground anywhere else.

As a part of the Sacrament ordinance, we receive a variety of spiritual gifts that, by themselves or taken as a whole, can be the antidote for the poisonous telestial tendencies that suppress the expression of celestial sureties.

In the Sacrament, the gift of the Holy Ghost is the fruit of the Spirit that we receive as we are taught the doctrine of Christ.

The Sacrament is of
such power that it drives the
law into our inward parts, so that
it is written upon our hearts. A mighty
change takes place as we experience the
process of sanctification. When we are
born again, the desired result of all
Gospel-oriented teaching has been
achieved, and we have no more
disposition to do evil, but to
do good continually. Our
faith is perfected in
the Sacrament.

The characteristics of Zion are simply the result of a spiritual transformation that takes place in the lives of those who avail themselves of the Sacrament on a regular basis.

The Sacrament
is far more than the
making of resolutions, that
are nothing more than promises to
ourselves that are generally kept for a
few days or weeks at best, before they are
abandoned and we return to our previously
held lifestyles. The ordinance has staying
power. Its basis is belief that is anchored
within the rich culture medium of faith,
repentance, baptism, and the steady
influence of the Holy Ghost.

The portal to Eden may have swung shut for us, but as it did, another door opened that introduced us to a a secret garden that is only accessible to those who grasp the awesome power of covenants.

We may live
in the world as long
as we plant our feet on
Gospel sod, and have attuned
our ears to eternity. The covenant
blesses us with the Spirit because we
need to be able to recognize sounding
brass and tinkling cymbals for what they
really are. It catalyzes a mystical and
metaphysical transformation wherein
we are figuratively born of God, so
that, with new eyes, we can see
more clearly, even all the
way to the gates of
heaven.

The Sacrament describes both the physical world and the forces that binds it together, stemming from the Divine. "Now wonder, ye angels," Charles Spurgeon wrote of the mortal mission of the Savior, "the Infinite has become an infant; He, upon whose shoulders the universe doth hang, nurses at his mother's breast; He who created all things, and bears up the pillars of creation."

The ordinance
of the Sacrament instills
within us a dawn of recognition
as we realize that we are the "elect
according to the foreknowledge of God
the Father, through sanctification of the
Spirit, unto obedience and sprinkling
of the blood of Jesus Christ."
(1 Peter 1:2).

The Apostle Paul observed of the Athenians, who were not so very different from ourselves, that they bowed down before unknown gods, whom they ignorantly worshipped. It is in the hope that we might be able to stand independently as witnesses of Jesus Christ, Who is the true and living God, that we participate in the ordinance of the Sacrament.

The key to liberation from our bondage to sin, that we might enjoy a freedom to become, is an adjustment in attitude that is reflected in our desire to participate in the ordinance of the Sacrament. To paraphrase Helen Keller, the real tragedy is not those of us who were born without sight, but those of us who have our sight, but do not have vision.

We partake of the Sacrament determined to follow the Savior "with full purpose of heart, acting no hypocrisy and no deception before God." (2 Nephi 31:13). As we do so, the night of darkness is followed by a renaissance, the spiritual rebirth that paves the way for enlightenment. Our new world blossoms with ideas and unbridled optimism. We realize that it is we to whom the prophet referred in Isaiah 9:2. Though we "walked in darkness, (we) have seen a great light. They that dwelt in the land of the shadow of death, upon them hath the light shined."

Pride is
motivated by self
will, while the Sacrament is
inspired by God's will. Pride is
driven by the fear of man, while
the Sacrament is nurtured by the
love of God. The applause of
the world rings loudly in the
ears of the proud, but it is
the accolades of heaven
that warm the hearts
of the faithful.

Those
who refuse the
Spirit's invitation
to partake of the
Sacrament have hard
hearts, stiff-necks, and
are overtly and covertly
rebellious. They lack the
malleability as well as
the pliability that one
needs to look up
to God, and
live.

After we
have submitted
to baptism, the Spirit
will teach us how to become
engaged in fashioning defensive
weapons in the armory of thought.
It is with these tools that the Lord
will show us just how we will be
able to construct the heavenly
fortifications of love, joy,
strength, and peace thru
the ordinance of the
Sacrament.

In our
anticipation of
the Sacrament, the
righteousness of our
efforts will be revealed
in spectacular simplicity
and plainness. The walls of
opposition to our purposeful
repentance will crumble and
fall away. In our exertion, the
Lord will comfort and succor
us with the bread of life. As we
journey through the harsh and
unforgiving environment of
Idumea, seeking the Lord
while He may be found,
oases will spring up
in the desert and
living water will
slake our
thirst.

If we ignore
the influences of
the Light of Christ and
the Holy Ghost that nurture
our innate urge to follow our
spiritual promptings to participate
in the Sacrament, but instead allow
ourselves to be distracted by trifling
concerns, we sin by omission and risk
settling for life in a marshland of
mediocrity that can degenerate
into a quicksand of sin, from
which there will be no
easy escape.

Sometimes,
it is only when
we have enrolled
in the graduate school
of hard knocks, and have
pre-paid the required tuition,
that we obtain the credits that
are earned by our obedience to the
curriculum. In the process, we learn
how to show charity to our brothers
and sisters, as a token of respect
to the performance cost that
is tied to our sacramental
covenant.

Our exercise of free will in an atmosphere of opposition propels us onward toward immortality and eternal life, as long as we rely on the twin ordinances of baptism and the Sacrament, as well as on the Atonement of Christ, to keep the sand of sin out of our gears.

The
Atonement
and the Sacrament
are the best fire insurance
policies we could have. They
indemnify us against being burned
as stubble at the last day. As long as
we pay our premiums, we will receive
the kinds of immortal bodies that
we will need in the resurrection,
so that we may dwell forever
in celestial burnings.

The
Sacrament
grounds us to
practical belief, but
its elements commit us
to an upward thrust.
It confirms that
we are known
to God.

If we could be participants in the spiritual equivalent of Weight Watchers, we would have less trouble sleeping, less difficulty focusing, and less of a problem faithfully attending Sacrament meeting.

Partaking of the
Sacrament is special,
because it introduces our
souls to rhythms in nature that
can only be felt when our behavior
is in harmony with eternal principles.
Thus, heaven always holds its breath as
it waits upon the initiative of those who
have been charged with the commission
to be good examples to others by
receiving the emblems
of Christ.

The ordinance of the Sacrament is only made possible because of the Atonement, which can save us from our natural state of carnality, sensuality, and devilish inclinations. It activates the Law of Mercy, which mitigates for those who conform to its requirements the effects of the first Law, that demands Justice. It lifts us to a state of holiness, spirituality, angelic innocence, and happiness. It prepares us to feel comfortable in our heavenly home, where we will find ourselves in the presence of angels softly singing celestial lullabies that express our love for the Savior.

The Sacrament means forsaking our carnal nature that is nothing more than a shadowy after image of Lucifer's rebellion at the Council in Heaven.

Our comprehension
of the sacramental covenant
flows easily and poetically to our
minds. Our persistence leads to practiced
fluency with the language of the Spirit that is the
inevitable result of the inspiration that comes as
we approach the ordinance with faith, fasting,
and prayer. As our minds are enlightened, we
are cast off into a stream of revelation
and carried along in the quickening
currents of direct experience
with the mind and
will of God.

Each time we partake of the Sacrament, through God's infinite goodness, and the manifestations of the Spirit, we have great views of that which is to come. The soothing emanation of familiar oscillations of energy resonating from within the limitless reserves that are selflessly shared by the Holy Ghost carry us along on rolling waves of the Spirit toward a more sure personal witness of the Savior's divinity and of His sacrifice.

We
partake of
the Sacrament,
so we might think
less in terms of self
sufficiency, and more
about Christ dependency.
We realize that His doctrine
is intended to change not
only our behavior, but
also our nature. We
are as putty in
His hands.

The Sacrament affirms the immortality of our souls, because within ourselves, we feel immortal longings. As we partake of the emblems of bread and water, we brush against the veil. We feel inner stirrings that are the harmonic vibrations of the music of heavenly choirs, and we hear the indistinct murmurings of the voices of angelic messengers.

After we have partaken of the Sacrament, we are no longer children, tossed to and fro on the sea of life. The covenant is God's promise that He will never leave us to fight our battles alone. Instead, we will always have His Spirit to be with us.

When we go
the second mile
while lengthening
our stride following
our Sacrament service,
we experience a freedom
that we had not known. We
are free of the shackles that
had limited the expression of
our potential and receive the
gift of spiritual independence
that disperses the darkness,
and removes the veil of
insensitivity to our
destiny.

When
we ponder
our sacramental
covenant, we beseech
the aid of the Spirit, that
we might thereafter be "slow
to be led to do iniquity, and
quick to hearken unto the words
of the Lord." (Helaman 7:7). There
needs to be opposition in all things,
but without help from above, we can
be seduced by the corrosive cocktails
of convenience that are cleverly
concocted by a bartender
named Beelzebub.

The principles of The
Plan carry us from baptism to
the covenant of the Sacrament. "For
behold, thus saith the Lord God: I will
give unto the children of men line upon
line, precept upon precept, here a little
and there a little. Blessed are those
who hearken unto my precepts, and
lend an ear unto my counsel, for
they shall learn wisdom; for
unto him that receiveth,
I will give more."
(2 Nephi 28:30).

The Sacrament
gives us perspective
to see adversity as a
diamond dust that can
polish us to a high luster,
rather than as an abrasive
that does nothing more
than wear us down
and grind us up.

The Sacrament
emancipates us from
the self-limiting conditions
that had heretofore blinded us
to a larger view of life. It frees us to
pay closer attention to celestial guideposts
and principles. It invites us to experience more
intense and reflective self-awareness, deeper
and more abiding humility, reinvigorated
confidence, and incomprehensively
more profound and enduring
faith that is quickened by
the Spirit.

The Sacrament imparts to us the opportunity to enjoy the best of both worlds; to live on the earth, to be sure, but to still wrap our spirits around a heavenly peace that surpasses understanding.

During our Sacrament services in particular, we feel the Spirit through the medium of music. We are reminded that even before the foundations of the earth were laid, there was a harmony in heaven that infused the celestial air; when the morning stars sang together, and all the sons and daughters of God shouted for joy.
(See Job 38:7).

We return again and again
to the Sacrament table because
none of us would choose to become
spiritually depleted, or to perish because
we had willfully neglected the very things
that matter the most. We understand the
consequences that inevitably follow our
doctrinal dehydration, our spiritual
starvation, and our intellectual
inhibition. Who knew that a
cup of water and a scrap
of bread could be so
powerful?

Because
of our sacramental
covenant, there will come
a day in the not too distant
future, when the atmosphere will
be pungent with a heavenly aether that
is punctuated by the melodious strains of
our native language. Every detail will be
just as we had imagined it would be,
including our appreciation of the
reassuring radiant heat from
a celestial fire kindled
beforehand by our
Father.

The ordinance of the Sacrament was not conceived to follow the receipt of signs from heaven. Our faith precedes the miracle. We must take a few steps into the darkness, and then the spiritual strong searchlight illuminates the way. Confirmation always flows along the pathway that has been created by faith.

During the
administration of
the emblems of Christ,
if we are very quiet, and
we listen very carefully, we
can hear the gentle rustling of
the wings of angels coming from
behind a slightly-parted veil. The
company of beings from the unseen
world sweeps the cobwebs from our
minds and opens up to our view
undreamed vistas of otherwise
inaccessible experience.

We partake
of the Sacrament
so that we might unite
ourselves with the mechanism
by which eternal principles are
communicated. The ordinance is
a manifestation of the practical
application of the ability of the
Holy Ghost to be a Revelator
and a Testator.

As
we partake of
the bread and water,
we have little inclination
to look back as we flee from
Sodom and Gomorrah. We leave
the ranks of those who comfortably
maintain their summer residence in
Babylon, even though everything
but junk mail is delivered to
their permanent home
address in Zion.

The Sacrament opens our hearts and our minds to a breathtaking expansion of understanding. As we practice a learning style that embraces the Spirit, we discover the pattern of heaven itself, and it becomes our norm.

Moses counseled the Israelites to build upon the Rock of their salvation. He urged them to "write (their covenants) upon the posts of (their) houses" and to "not appear before the Lord empty" handed. (Deuteronomy 6:9 & 16:16). We would do well to do likewise, by remembering our covenant in the Sacrament, as we take upon ourselves His name, keep His commandments, and always remember Him.

In the
Sacrament, the
power of godliness is
unmistakable. And without
the authority of the priesthood
that administers the ordinance,
the power of godliness is not
manifest, even unto those
who profess to know
Jesus Christ on
every other
level.

May we so live
that we are never more
than a week away from the
last time we have partaken of
the Sacrament; so that when it is
time for heaven to reach out and
sweep us up into its embrace, we
will be prepared to respond in
kind, with open arms and
an engaging smile on
our face.

Those who speak in Sacrament meeting, do so following the administration of the emblems of Christ, when the covenant is fresh in the minds of their listeners. Therefore, they are always sure to maintain the focus of the meeting and their message on the Savior, and on His commandments, as they are directed by the Spirit.

We are not, and
never wish to be, lights
unto ourselves. We cannot
overcome the world on our own.
But when, in the Sacrament, we borrow
the Lord's strength and power, we can do
all things. Many times, He told disobedient
Israel that His "hand is stretched out still."
(Isaiah 10:4). If we ignore it, or if we
refuse His invitation to lift us up, we
invite disaster. Our behavior must
foster the power of humility, for
it is the meek who shall
inherit the earth.

The road that
leads to the Sacrament
table takes us through the
portal of personal preparedness,
accountability, and responsibility,
in the direction of celestial sureties
that have not only been encompassed
by an expanding circle of opportunity,
but that have also been embraced by the
perfect law of liberty. Our covenants, and
in particular the privilege of partaking
of the Sacrament, make us feel as if
we have been born again, through a
spiritual birth canal that delivers
us into the Lord's Rest and
eternal life.

As we embrace the
power of the Sacrament,
we are blessed with visions
of the Celestial Kingdom that
dance before our eyes. Our faith
in the Savior moves us closer to
heaven's gate. We first seek the
kingdom and His righteousness.
We have learned that when our
priorities are guided by the
Spirit, we need not fear
for want of our most
basic needs.

If we have done as
the Lord has commanded,
our comprehension of emblems
of the Sacrament will flow easily and
poetically to our minds. Our persistence
and our participation will lead to practiced
fluency with the language of the Spirit that is
the result of the inspiration that will come as
we approach the ordinance with faith, fasting,
and prayer. As our minds are enlightened, we
will be cast off into a stream of revelation
and carried along in the quickening
currents of direct experience
with the mind and
will of God.

The
Sacrament
encourages us to
be faithful, with an
emphasis on the "ful."
In its abundance, we find
there is more than enough,
even a surplus, a surfeit, that
brims over with possibilities; even
overflows with options that we may
have never before considered. If our
cup seems to run over as we consider
our blessings during the administration
of the ordinance, it is because that is
how Heavenly Father designed it to
be, for the Spirit to shepherd us
right into the embrace
of eternity.

The
ordinance
of the Sacrament
can direct the course
of the circumstances in
which we find ourselves. First,
we pre-play, and then, we re-play.
Our anticipation of success prepares
us to deal with the adversity and the
setbacks that will surely come to each
of us. We believe in divine design. When
we dismiss the promised blessings that
are found in the Sacrament, we are
guilty of turning away our faces
from the habitation
of the Lord.

When
we partake of the
Sacrament, we commemorate
the rebirth of our immortal souls.
Bathed in stunning light, those who
participate stare in wide-eyed wonder
at the beautiful simplicity of the threads
that have been woven into a pattern
of principles that become a vibrant
embroidery of simple ordinances
that are performed under the
guidance of God's holy
priesthood.

During our
Sacrament service,
we enjoy the guidance
of the Holy Ghost, which
teaches the peaceable things
of the kingdom. We matriculate
into a curriculum where we learn
by repetition to understand with
fluency the language of
the Spirit.

We partake
of the Sacrament
that we might rejoice
in our characterization by
others as peculiar people, for,
in our eyes, we have become
witnesses to the vitalization
of the Merciful Plan of
our Creator.

The
Sacrament
endows us with
the strength to watch
ourselves judiciously, to
be the meticulous guardians
of our thoughts, the scrupulous
custodians of our words, and the
prudent caretakers of our deeds, to
fastidiously observe the commandments
of God, to continue evenly in the faith,
and to endure in righteousness. That
is a tall order, but the ordinance
of the Sacrament empowers us
to stand above the crowd
and to exceed our
expectations.

Bathed in the stunning clarity of light, those who have partaken of the bread and water often stare in wide-eyed wonder at the beautiful simplicity of the interwoven threads within the pattern of principles that make up the tapestry of our Sacrament services.

Evidence of the exercise
of our faith is revealed in how
we receive the Sacrament. We gain
spiritual maturity until our faith becomes
perfect knowledge. Initially, faith is to believe
what we do not see, and the reward of faith is
to see what we believe. The process by which
faith is developed is one of testing. The
Lord gives certain principles, and by
obedience to them, blessings
and power follow.

During
the administration
of the Sacrament, we
turn our thoughts to the
Savior without distraction,
that we might feel His energy
building within us, until it lifts us
to the zenith of experience where
the lines distinguishing mortality
from eternity blur, and we find
ourselves consumed in a fire
of everlasting burnings, as
we come face to face
with eternity thru
the influence of
the Spirit.

The bread and water help us to comfortably memorize our lines in the Three Act Play that has a noteworthy title: The Plan of Salvation.

The Sacrament open
up windows of opportunity
to better understand the principles
of the Gospel, that remain as mysteries
to those who have not spiritually prepared
themselves for personal revelation from God.
The Lord has assured us that we "shall know
of a surety that these things are true,
for from heaven will (He) declare
it unto (us)." (D&C 5:12).

There are no shades of grey after we have received the ordinance of the Sacrament. Our thoughts become "single to God." (D&C 88:68). If we try to have it both ways, our double mindedness will create intellectual instability and spiritual schizophrenia, for we cannot be servants of the Devil while pretending to follow Christ.

"The harder the conflict, the more glorious the triumph. What we obtain too cheap, we esteem too lightly; 'tis dearness only that gives everything its value. Heaven knows how to put a proper price upon its goods." (Tom Paine, "Common Sense"). It would be strange, indeed, if such a celestial article as the Sacrament should not be highly rated.

The worth of the
principles of the Gospel
is validated through personal
witness, or testimony. Our desire
to participate in the ordinance of the
Sacrament becomes the outward expression
of our personal dedication to obedience. It
is the public manifestation of our yearning to
enjoy a private covenant relationship with
God. In order for that happen, we must
voluntarily surrender our agency to a
higher power, and subjugate our
ambition to His will.

Because of the Sacrament, we are liberated from our self defeating behaviors. Obedience to Gospel principles blesses us to "be like the bird who, pausing in her flight awhile on boughs too light, feels them give way beneath her, and yet sings, knowing she hath wings." (Victor Hugo).

We take
the Sacrament
that we might know
that we are here, at this
time, and in this place, by
divine design. What we think
are merely coincidences, when
they are viewed thru the clarifying
lens of eternity, are faith promoting
examples of the Lord patiently working
behind the scenes in our behalf. Nothing
in this life happens by chance. Everything
of significance happens by divine design.
We receive the Sacrament as a testament
that "the works, and the designs, and
the purposes of God cannot be
frustrated, neither can they
come to naught."
(D&C 3:1).

We take
the Sacrament
that we might have
opportunities to bear
each other's burdens. We
do not consider the merits
of the petitions of the weak
and impoverished who need
our aid and we turn a blind
eye to prejudices that might
threaten to influence the
depth and breadth of
our compassion.

We partake of the Sacrament, that we might "be full of the knowledge of the Lord, as the waters cover the sea." (Isaiah 11:9). The ordinance of the Sacrament promises to leave the world a better place than it was beforehand.

For
The Plan
to succeed,
there needs to
be opposition; light
and darkness, pleasure
and pain, good and evil,
and happiness and misery,
which makes the Sacrament
essential. Most of us lack the
spiritual horsepower to choose
the right consistently, much less
to save ourselves. It is safe to
say that we need God every
hour of every day of
our lives.

When
we partake
of the Sacrament,
we sense the peace
of God, which surpasses
our understanding. We are
given the opportunity to enjoy
the best of both worlds; to live
on earth, but still have a place
where we can retreat from the
turmoil of the world. We sit
in a holy place when we
participate together in
the ordinance of the
Sacrament.

We
partake of
the Sacrament that
we might be perfected in
our Savior, Jesus Christ. Our
spiritual awakening progresses
for just as long as we are learning.
We take solace in the scriptures, where,
although we are admonished 154 times
to be perfect, we are also encouraged
129 times to "learn" and 995 times
simply to "begin." As D&C 29:22
suggests, we "begin to be
redeemed."

Those who partake of the Sacrament "in obedience to the commandments, shall receive health in their navel and marrow to their bones; and shall find wisdom and great treasures of knowledge, even hidden treasures; and shall run and not be weary, and shall walk and not faint."(D&C 89:18).

Blind
opposition, hostility,
inflexibility, intolerance
enmity and hatred, are the
raw and ugly manifestations of
pride, but these are overwhelmed
by the accommodation, charity,
faith, approachability, hope,
and sociability of those
who partake of the
Sacrament in
faith.

The Sacrament nurtures our relationship with our Heavenly Father and with the Holy Ghost, while, at the same time, the Savior becomes the fashioner of our fortunes.

As
we prepare
ourselves for the
Sacrament, angels
will attend us. "For I
will go before your face,"
promised the Savior. "I will
be on your right hand, and on
your left, and my Spirit shall be
in your hearts, and mine angels
round about you, to bear you up."
(D&C 84:88). With such a promise,
how could we think to turn our
backs on such reinforcement,
return to our wicked ways,
and elect to go it alone?
The thought makes
reason stare.

The Sacrament, that relies on the Atonement of Christ, is the only fire retardant that can be dumped onto the raging inferno of sin.

For as long as we tarry
on the earth, we will remain
subject to the effects of adversity
and of opposition, and without the
therapeutic benefits of the Sacrament,
we must needlessly suffer from a stiff
neck that prevents us from looking up
to Heavenly Father for guidance, over
to our leaders for counsel, around
to seek out those who are in need,
and down in an attitude of
modesty, humility, and
of contrition.

Without purposeful repentance followed by baptism and the Sacrament, we cannot reasonably expect to inherit the glory of celestial realms; especially if we have been agreeable to abide by only telestial or terrestrial principles that put fewer demands upon our discipleship.

In lieu of the Sacrament, and if we do not repent, the Holy Spirit, which has the capacity to burn as a fire, must be quenched, and the Atonement will lose its power to save us from our sins.

The Sacrament is a difficult principle for some to grasp because it was conceived in heaven. It is not of this world, and so if they try to wrap their finite minds around it, they will never succeed in doing so. It is spiritually discerned.

Lucifer fell from heaven with a deafening thud. We feel its after-shock even today, if we decline the invitation to receive the Spirit.

If we hope to successfully deal with the inequalities of life and escape the quicksands of self-pity, we must personalize the lessons of the Atonement, and that is best accomplished during the sweet hour of prayer that is found in Sacrament meeting.

It is
in our hearts
that we determine to
receive the Sacrament. We
are humbled, as we receive
chastisement and counsel. We
forgive those who have offended
us. We render service, and our
good example teaches others
that blessings will follow us
when we do as Heavenly
Father would have
us do.

God knows
what is best and
has confidence in
our divine potential to
to develop His nature. He
commands us to repent, be
baptized, develop faith, and
invite the Spirit to guide us, thru
the Sacrament. Because these goals
are well within our reach, they become
the foundation of the requirements that
must be met if we hope, one day, to gain
readmittance to the Celestial Kingdom
of heaven.

Only with
the Sacrament, does
mortality become the
wonderful center for the
talented and gifted that
it was envisioned to
be, by the Merciful
Plan of our
Father.

Repentance, made possible by the Atonement and the Sacrament, removes the stain of sin from the tapestry that is the tableau of our lives.

No matter
how ponderous
the burden is that we
have created due to our
inattention to our spiritual
well-being, after purposeful
repentance, the Sacrament,
or more accurately, the
Spirit, will lift us up
at the last day.

The Sacrament gives us the means to reset our spiritual appestats when we notice they are out of whack, and we find ourselves indulging, and even binge eating, in sin, which thing we never before had supposed might happen.

Unless our behavior during Sacrament meeting is in harmony with the laws of the Gospel, our unrestrained freedom must inevitably lead to bondage at the hands of the Devil.

In the Atonement, as well as in the Sacrament, our craving to be clean finds its expression in celestial sparks that ignite our desire to continually repent.

Ghostbusters
may find themselves
slimed as they interact
with the forces of evil, but
those who mingle among the
Saints in Sacrament meeting are
destined to be covered in stardust
as they rub shoulders with the Spirit.

When the
Sacrament is
the fuel firing
our determination
to follow the Savior,
His Atonement charges
our spiritual batteries as
it energize our vision with
an infinite perspective.
We can become holy
and without
spot.

Thank God for the ordinance of the Sacrament that helps us to get thru each day, and comforts us during every long night of darkness, throughout our lives. Truly, God stays up late and leaves a light burning for us, to guide us back Home.

The Church
was restored so
that latter-day Israel
might receive the Gospel
and enter into covenants of
salvation and justification, as
well as those of sanctification
and exaltation; and that by the
authority of the priesthood of
God the Sacrament might be
administered to all who
qualify by worthiness
to partake of the
emblems of
Christ.

Christ reconciles "the world unto himself, not imputing their trespasses unto them; and hath committed unto us the word of reconciliation" through the administration of the ordinance of the Sacrament of the Lord's Supper. (2 Corinthians 5:18-19).

Our Heavenly Father blesses us with the ordinance of the Sacrament because He is able to envision the worst circumstances in which we will find ourselves. He has pre-played, and now we are replaying, the drama of our lives. When He declared: "We will prove them herewith, to see if they will do all things whatsoever the Lord their God shall command them," it was as much a statement of fact as it was a question of whether or not we would be obedient. (Abraham 3:25).

The ordinance of
the Sacrament is a great
place to learn the grammar of
the Gospel. It is the exclamation
point of our repentance process. We
approach the ordinance with confidence
that "at the banquet of consequences,
we will be able to bow our heads in
reverence, rather than hang them
in shame, in the presence of
God who will be there."
(Marion D. Hanks).

We partake of the Sacrament at the start of a week that is sure to have its ups and downs. In its administration, there is consistency. It provides a bastion of stability in the midst of the turmoil of the world. It has a powerful and influential capacity to center our hearts, might, mind, and strength on our covenant relationship with Heavenly Father, Jesus Christ, and the Holy Ghost.

As
we ponder
the Sacrament,
let us remember that
the Savior is our life-line,
providing security when our
footing is unsure and the foaming
sea is streaming across the deck. He is
our compass, showing us the way, especially
when the course before us is unclear. He is our
chart that warns us of hidden dangers. He is our
barometer, alerting us to impending storms. He is
our lookout, standing as our sentinel when we
are distracted by trivial concerns. He holds
the line that trails in our wake, offering
safety should we lose our footing and
fall overboard. He is the wind that
fills our sails, that we may
find our way home.

There is no fanfare in the Sacrament; just quiet reflection, meditation, contemplation, introspection, and a deep desire to draw near to our Father. Though our flesh and our hearts may fail, God is our strength and our portion forever.

Our active participation in the Sacrament helps us to see things as they really are, and at the same time, it compels us to be benevolently blind to the shortcomings of others. Just so, Heavenly Father is blind to our own failures when we come to the Sacrament table having completed the arduous process of repentance.

If we ignore
the blessings of the
Sacrament, we are guilty
of turning away our faces from
the habitation of the Lord. Because
the people of Judah disregarded both
the temple and its related ordinances,
2 Chronicles 29:8 reveal that the wrath
of the Lord was upon them and upon
Jerusalem, and He "delivered them
to trouble, to astonishment,
and to hissing."

The Sacrament
teaches us to engage
the gears of the engine
that drives us toward the
achievement of our goals. It
prevents us from remaining at a
stand-still with our transmission
idling in neutral, and being left
to wonder why we are not being
magically propelled forward
with no effort on our
own part.

As we turn our attention
to the scriptures, to fasting, to
prayer, to the Sacrament, and to an
active discipline-based lifestyle, we are
more likely to make progress as we follow
the Rod of Iron toward the Tree of Life. If
we falter in our faith during the journey, we
remember the word of the Lord to Israel:
"I will heal their backsliding, I will
"love them freely: for mine
anger is turned away."
(Hosea 14:4).

How we embrace
the Sacrament determines
how we handle our weaknesses,
our imperfections, and sin. Without
it, our self-defeating behaviors always
threaten to impede our progress. Because
the covenant of the Sacrament establishes
a partnership with our Heavenly Father, the
Savior, and the Holy Ghost, we can turn
the tables on Satan, and actually use
our inadequacies, blemishes, and
even our transgression, as our
own personal stepping-stones
to higher achievement.

The faithful
need not fear,
although they "see
signs and wonders, for
they shall be shown forth
in the heavens above, and in
the earth beneath. And they shall
behold blood, and fire, and vapors
of smoke." (D&C 45:40-41). Although
the spiritual equivalents of lightning
may strike all around them, they
will be shielded from harm by
the Sacrament's copper grid
that surrounds them and
and grounds them to
the Savior.

Spiritual preparation prior to receiving the emblems of the Sacrament readies us to complete the arduous process of our repentance. However, we do not partake of the Sacrament in order to receive a remission of sins, but rather to recommit ourselves to the promises we made at baptism. We receive by covenant the Spirit of God so that, in the future, we might more securely hold fast to the iron rod. We should only permit ourselves to partake of the Sacrament when we have beforehand completed the process of proper prior personal preparation, as a result of our repentance. Poor performance is thus prevented when we finally invite the Spirit to be with us, as part of the covenant we make with God in the Sacrament.

Our Father
in Heaven envisions
that we might one day
be like Him, and offers us
the Sacrament, to help us
get a taste of what He
has, as well as of
what He is.

The
priesthood of
God energizes His
grace as the Sacrament
is administered, allowing us
to receive blessings by binding
us to Him thru revelation by the
means of a covenant of action.
Because Heavenly Father honors
the principle of free will, our
progression patiently waits
upon our initiative.

The Law of Compensation
defines the behavior of those
who worthily partake of the emblems
of Christ. They observe the Golden Rule.
"Therefore all things whatsoever ye would
that men should do to you, do ye even
so to them: for this is the law and
the prophets." (Matthew 7:12).

Those who
decline the offer of
the riches of eternity that
might have been unfolded to
their view through the power of
the Sacrament are doomed to eke
out a subsistence level of existence in
scarcity of their basic spiritual needs.
With the smorgasbord of life spread
out before them, they settle for the
processed factory food that is
dished out by the automats
of the world. They live
beneath the poverty
level, and are not
even aware
of it.

When we partake of the
emblems of Christ, the doctrines
of the kingdom, or the solemnities
of eternity, are positioned right in the
forefront of our conscious awareness. We
take our understanding as far as our
capacity allows us to go, because it
is tailored to suit our individual
circumstances, and yet it is
collectively understood
and is universally
applicable.

If we want to receive the blessing of the covenant of the Sacrament, to "always have His spirit to be with us," we need to experience how the Holy Ghost manifests personal revelation. "For God speaketh once, yea twice, yet man perceiveth it not. In a dream, in a vision of the night, when deep sleep falleth upon men, in slumberings upon the bed; then he openeth the ears of men, and sealeth their instruction."
(Job 33:4-16).

As we partake of the Sacrament, we are blessed with several quiet minutes when we can think of the Savior in new and symbolic ways. He is, after all, the rudder of our ship, guiding us past unseen rocks and reefs. He is our helm, holding steady when winds of adversity blow. He is our telltale, alerting us to impending storms. He is our keel, helping us to move against the current and the wind. He is our mainsheet, holding firmly with just enough pressure to prevent us from capsizing when we are dangerously heeled over.

The bread and water are as the mortar that holds together the building blocks of character. Partaking of the Sacrament is the consummate compilation of affirmative action.

The Sacrament
is all-encompassing in its
scope. There are no height or weight
restrictions, no social, economic, cultural,
intellectual, or emotional prerequisites,
and no ecclesiastical qualifications,
other than membership in The
Church of Jesus Christ of
Latter-day Saints.

The gentle
influence of the
Spirit is woven into the
tapestry of the Sacrament.
For example, we are struck
by how deliberately the powers
of heaven are invoked in our
behalf, as we listen to the
words of the prayer.

At the Sacrament table, as before holy altars in the temple, we make sacred covenants with God, the fulfillment of which will bring us earthly blessings and eternal exaltation. As we focus our attention on worthiness to partake of the Sacrament, our thirst for truth will be quenched with the living water provided by the Gospel of Jesus Christ.

Just as water from
the spring of Gihon was
vital to the physical survival
of King Hezekiah's people during
the Assyrian conflict, living water is
essential for our spiritual survival
as we struggle with Satan. We are
under siege throughout our lives,
and constant access to living
water is our only hope
of salvation.

If we really desire to
have His Spirit to be with us during
our Sacrament meeting, we might want
to put away our tablets, and turn off our
cell phones, even if we have them on vibrate.
Instead of answering email, we might instead
quietly use our time seeking answers to our
prayers. Instead of searching for a strong
Wi-Fi signal, we could silently turn to the
scriptures, and allow the Holy Ghost
to guide us to powerful messages
from Ne-Phi and the other
prophets.

The gentle Spirit
that is nurtured during our
Sacrament services quietly prompts
us to ratchet down the hectic pace of
our lives. It calms our souls and carries us
away, far from the madding crowd. The Lord
knows how busy we are. He knows how it feels
to be neglected, to be ignored, and to be in a
fierce competition with telestial trivialities,
sounding brass, and tinkling cymbals. In
fact, He may have been thinking of the
Sacrament when He said: "Be still,
and know that I am God."
(Psalms 46:10).

In Sacrament
meeting, during an
hour of worship that takes
us far from the tumult of the
teeming multitudes and the telestial
crowds that so often characterize the
lifestyle of the rich and famous, the Holy
Ghost invites us sit back and let His Spirit
wash over the wrinkles in our spirits, to be
rejuvenated by a full facial and whole
body massage, that we might reflect
the image and likeness of God
in our countenances.

The symbolism of the
Lord's Last Supper has been
beautifully preserved for us in
the scriptures. (See John 13:1-35).
In accordance with revelation, the
ordinance of the Sacrament has been
restored. Broken bread represents the
torn flesh of the Savior, and the water
represents His blood that was shed in
His sacrifice and atonement
for our sins.

The ordinance of the Sacrament opens up channels of power that release the resources of the Holy Ghost so that our promised blessings might be fully realized. James Talmage taught: "The Sacrament has not been established as a specific means of securing any special blessing, aside from that of a continuing endowment of the Holy Spirit."

It is the
ordinance of the
Sacrament that orients
our sight so that it rests on
the stars, no matter where we may
be bobbing about on the ocean of life.
Initially, getting a fix on the symbolism
of the Gospel that comes alive for us with
intentional imagery and magical metaphor
might seem daunting. However, it won't be
long before the messages that have come
down to us from the ages will be easily
plotted by the Savior's sextant, that
finds form and substance in
the Sacrament.

It is in the
covenant of the
Sacrament that we are
given the tools we will need
to experience God's Rest. As we
wend our way through this vale of
tears, the real journey to Christ has
only just begun. In the Sacrament, we
lay aside things which had besought us,
that threatened to bring us down to our
destruction. We do this that we might
embrace things of a better and
more enduring substance.

We partake
of the Sacrament
that we might have
hope in our Savior. It
invites us to consider the
possibility that we might one
day be like Him. We believe that
His grace, that is embodied in the
Sacrament, consists of the gifts and
power by which we may be brought
to His perfection and stature, so
that we may enjoy not only
what He has, but also
what He is.

The Sacrament,
is God's invitation to
write our own chapter of
The Greatest Story Ever Told.
It is during the service that we
realize gone are the days when
we would have been content to
do nothing more than build
upon the sepulchres of
our fathers.

We receive the Sacrament that the Spirit of the Lord Omnipotent might work "a mighty change in us, or in our hearts, that we have no more disposition to do evil, but to do good continually." (Mosiah 5:2).

We receive
the Sacrament
"through the infinite
goodness of God, that
by the manifestations of
his Spirit we might have great
views of that which is to come.
Rather than multiplying mirrors
by only studying angles without
thinking to increase the light,
the Sacrament illuminates
our minds through the
inexhaustible power
of the Spirit.

The
Sacrament
invigorates our
actions and charges
our spiritual batteries.
It energizes our vision
with infinite perspective,
creating pulsing streams
of insight, intuition,
inspiration, and
revelation.

After
the Sacrament,
we return to the real
world, to be sent forth as
sheep in the midst of wolves.
We have been provided a shield
of protection against the spatter of
corrosive perspiration cast off by the
destroyer, who, we learn, will work
overtime to damage our doctrinal
defenses, diminish our charitable
capacity, deplete our bountiful
reservoirs of sympathy, dull
our spiritual sensitivities,
and destroy our
devotions.

When we partake of the Sacrament, the cobwebs are swept from our minds, and we are blessed with the visitation of the Holy Ghost, which does nothing short of filling us with hope and perfect love.

After the
administration
of the Sacrament,
we press forward, not
with the crowd who jostles
for position in the circus of
telestial trivialities, but instead
with those who seek wisdom as they
strive to comprehend the mysteries
of God. We get a fix on eternity
when we focus our attention on
the Star of the greatest show
on earth, Who is Jesus
Christ.

As we
partake of the
bread and water,
our faith is anchored
upon the foundation of
rock, rather than sand. Our
testimonies are composed of
three essential elements. First
is our conscious recognition of
Gospel principles. Second is our
understanding of the Lord's word
concerning the principles. Finally,
is our direct experience with the
principles, which is what we call
"the fruits of faith." Some have
explained this experience as
a mystical spiritual rapture
that occurs during the
administration of
the Sacrament.

We partake
of the Sacrament
that we might learn
how to consecrate to
the Lord our time, our
talents, our means, and
all else with which He
has providently
blessed our
lives.

The
tangible token
of our acceptance
of our Father's invitation
to join Him in His work and
glory, which is to bring to pass
our immortality and eternal life,
is the ordinance of the Sacrament.
Some may consider the commitment
too costly, but countless witnesses
have testified how obedience has
become, for them, the perfect
law of liberty.

During the administration of the Sacrament, when our souls have been illuminated by the glow that emanates from the burning Spirit of God, we can no longer remain passive. There is a flickering fire of faith that warms our souls as we begin to recognize the upward reach within ourselves. We are sensitized to truth, to beauty, and to a goodness above and beyond our our own attainment. If we are fortunate, we experience the faint stirrings of the golden quality of gratitude.

In the
ordinance of
the Sacrament we
adopt a culture of
faith that embraces us,
to help insulate us from
worldly influences. It alerts
us to Satan's misdirection, that
attempts to lead us from brilliant,
dazzling white, through every shade
of grey, to that fathomless black which,
by subtraction, is the absence of every
uplifting thought, word, deed, or
sustaining principle.

When we are tempted to curse the darkness, it is the Sacrament that invites us to pause, and instead light a candle.

In the
Sacrament,
we measure
the distance to
the heavens in faith
and not in miles. It is
not a question of dollars
and cents, but rather of
the quality of our
commitment to
the Lord.

We partake
of the Sacrament
that we be no longer
carried about by every wind
of doctrine, which are worldly
influences that play mind-games
with us as they jockey for position
in a competition for market share
in the flea markets of Babylon.

Every day of our lives, the Spirit influences us to choose liberty and eternal life, instead of captivity and spiritual death. We choose to live our lives within the framework of the Sacrament. Without it, unbridled freedom would inevitably lead to tyranny. We are free to choose whether or not we wish to participate in the Sacrament, but we cannot escape the consequences, if we choose unwisely.

The Sacrament opens up a portal to the principles, ordinances, and covenants that enable us to be sanctified, to be worthy to live again in a state of holiness in the presence of our Heavenly Father. Because of the Sacrament, we "continue in the supplicating of his grace," to one day stand blameless before Him at His Pleasing Bar. (Alma 7:3).

The Sacrament is the great equalizer for all of Heavenly Father's children. The ordinances that illuminate The Plan will always stand ready to save our souls, but in the meantime, the children of God may worship Him according to the dictates of their own conscience. He will force no one to heaven.

The Sacrament is the
catalyst that propels us upward
toward our discovery of the personal
levels of our experience with the Savior.
For when we talk of knowing Him, we are
referring to a special sense of the word. It
is not enough to know about Him by reading
the Gospels, or by listening to others speak
of Him. We must know Him thru the bonds
of common experience and feeling, and
therein lies the beauty and the power
of the Sacrament to touch lives
with the fire of faith.

A
conduit
to living water
is created when we not
only believe, but also act on
our belief, by being honest, true,
chaste, benevolent, virtuous, kind,
and in doing good to others.
The Sacrament fortifies us
to internalize these
characteristics.

We can
turn to no-one but
God for the assurance that
liberates us from fear, doubt, the
apprehension of danger, the turmoil
of the world, and from the vagaries of
men. Only when we have cast off the self-
limiting conditions and the self-defeating
behaviors that had blinded us to a larger
view of life, will we be able to enjoy a
settled conviction of the truth in
our minds. We will partake of
the emblems of Christ with
a renewed faith.

As we think about the Savior, we intuitively respond to President Gordon B. Hinckley's invitation to do a little better, to be a little more kind, to be a little more merciful, and a little more forgiving; "to put behind us our weaknesses of the past, and go forth with new energy and increased resolution to improve the world about us, whether it be in our homes, in our places of employment, or in our social activities."

During the administration of the Sacrament, we feel the word enlarge our souls and enlighten our understanding. As Brigham Young said: "Every Gospel principle carries within it a witness that it is true." In the economy of the Gospel, "we often catch a spark from the awakened memories of the immortal soul, which lights up our whole being as with the glory of our former home." (Joseph F. Smith).

The world attempts to change us from the outside, and fails miserably. The Sacrament changes us from the inside, and succeeds brilliantly. We are thus created to reach our potential in both the image and the likeness of God, our Father.

The Sacrament
creates within our hearts
a groundswell of emotions
that generate the passion to lift
us to heaven. Our worship becomes
more vibrant and dynamic than the
mechanical observance of a variety of
ceremonial rules, because it's energy
helps us to capture emotion, contour
attitude, crystalize thought, congeal
passion, compartmentalize action,
communicate feeling, and convey
sentiments, in ways that influence
the creation of an atmosphere
within which our spiritual
revitalization may
occur.

Righteousness is always modest in its appearance, but it looks so good on us in our Sacrament meeting!

As we live in a harmonious
relationship with the principles of
the Gospel, we begin to understand
how our covenants with God help us to
overcome adversity and gain self-mastery.
We learn how God's promises can help us
to focus our efforts to become as He is.
With a quickening pulse, we begin to
understand that the ordinance of
the Sacrament prepares us to
become as God is.

In the final analysis, our righteous objective is to conduct our lives so that the Holy Ghost may justify us, and find that we have been perfectly obedient to the covenant of the Sacrament. This enables Heavenly Father to welcome us into His Rest. His promised blessing has the power to move us along the path of progression to the point that we internalize His divine nature so that we might be at ease in His presence. This is one of the reasons why we repetitively rehearse, not only the Sacrament, but also the veil experience in the temple.

It is at
the Sacrament table
that we matriculate into a
curriculum where we learn to
understand the language spoken
by the Holy Ghost. It is there that
we happily pay the price to receive
the antidote for poisonous telestial
tendencies that are always lurking
about and threatening to choke
the expression of celestial
sureties.

The ordinance of the Sacrament activates the redemption exemption that is a codicil to the Law of Justice, as our lease on life is renegotiated to our advantage by the Atonement of Jesus Christ.

The gulf that exists between Saints and sinners matters very little, for at the end of the day, the Sacrament is the great equalizer. In the ordinance, we see how our Heavenly Father is no respecter of persons.

During Sacrament
service, when we are in
the company of the community
of Christ, we catch a religious fever
that elevates our testimony temperature
enough to get our juices flowing with an
appreciation of Who the Savior really is.
Only then, will we experience the earth
shaking and mind bending theophany
that we are His spiritual offspring.
Only then, will we recognize the
awesome potential of our
position.

We can have no proof of the promise of the Sacrament to bless us with the Spirit, until we act on the basis of our belief. Then comes ratification, manifest as a spiritual confirmation, but only after we have exercised faith. This is why James taught that "faith, if it hath not works, is dead, being alone." (James 2:17).

Every day of the week, and not just on Sunday, we make the choice to receive the Sacrament, or not to do so. Our decision may be illuminated by our discipleship. On the other hand, it may be determined by the darkness of the Devil.

Without the Atonement of Christ and devoid of the blessings we receive because of our obedience to our covenants, we must forever remain miserable, living in an unrelenting state of separation from the presence of our Heavenly Father, His Son Jesus Christ, and the Holy Ghost.

Temporal baggage
can create imbalance
that leads to confusion.
The Sacrament jars us out
of our collective complacency
by upsetting the stagnation of the
status quo. It invites us to enjoy a
settled conviction by getting us moving,
prodding us to constructively expend our
energy, and putting our agency to work,
that we might claim the blessing of the
Spirit as we take upon ourselves the
name of Jesus Christ, promise to
to remember Him, and keep all
of His commandments.

The ordinance
of the Sacrament brings
us close enough to heaven
to grasp its riches, by expanding
upon our vision. We move beyond
physical laws that pertain only to the
temporal world, toward an appreciation
of Gospel principles that relate to the
eternities. It explains exactly what we
must do if we wish to reach out and
touch the face of God. The path
that lies before us is clear.
There is no variableness,
neither is there even a
hint of turning.

The words of the sacrament prayer encourage us to step back, to take a deep breath, pause for a moment, and ponder the next important steps in our busy lives. The covenant tenderly familiarizes us with the warm embrace of daily spiritual experiences that will help us to keep our priorities straight.

It is a harsh reality that as
our circle of knowledge grows,
so do the borders of darkness that
encroach upon the edge of the light.
The more we know, the more we need
to learn, that we might better deal with
the opposition that is a part of all of
our undertakings. In the Sacrament,
we are centered. It orients us to
the light, so that the shadows
will always be behind us.

It is because of the
Sacrament that we leave
the world a better place than
when we found it. It prepares us to
pass through the veil. Because of it, when
we finally do so, we will leave with those we
have left behind legacies of both tangible and
intangible remembrances. We will leave them
with our testimonies. We will leave them with
gratitude for the privilege and blessing to
have been knit together as a family that
was able to pause in its busy schedule
and follow the path to the Sacrament
table each and every Sabbath day.

Sometimes, when we brush
against the veil, we feel the stirrings
that are the harmonic vibrations of the
music of a heavenly choir, and we hear the
indistinct murmurings of the voices of angelic
messengers. This is one of the reasons that we
partake of the Sacrament; that while we yet
dwell on the earth, we might be blessed
to become the partakers of the divine
nature of our Heavenly Father.

The
indescribable peace
that follows obedience to
the covenant of the Sacrament
nudges the intangible evidence of
a greater spiritual reality within our
reach. When we realize that we are not
alone, we will have begun a journey
that carries us to a higher state of
being where we will find ourselves
covered in star dust as we rub
shoulders with the Gods.

The
Spirit throws
open the windows
of our souls to let in
more light, so that we might
better understand the principles
that drive the Sacrament forward.
These are mysteries to those who have
not prepared themselves for the streams
of revelation that come from God. The
Lord has assured us, however, that we
"shall know of a surety that these
things are true, for from heaven
will (He) declare it" unto us.
(D&C 5:12).

There are no shades of grey after we have received the ordinance of the Sacrament. Our thoughts become "single to God." (D&C 88:68). If we try to have it both ways, our double mindedness will create intellectual instability and spiritual schizophrenia, for we cannot be servants of the Devil while pretending to follow Christ.

Partaking of the emblems of Christ helps us to be patient in our afflictions. Exercising our faith that the Holy Ghost will be with us until the end of our days helps us as we endure our trials and tribulations, even when they are undeserved, or when we cannot understand why they have been given to us.

It is during the
Sacrament that we feel
the gentle caress of the hands
of the Master Potter, as He turns our
lives with the hand of time. We give Him
permission, as the Artisan of our destiny, to
mold us and shape us. (See Jeremiah 18:6). We
are the clay, and He is our potter; and we are
the work of His hands. (See Isaiah 64:8). As
our thoughts turn to the Savior, we remain
impressionable and pliable as the Holy
Ghost sculpts us into new creatures
in Christ. We see that it is our
destiny to personify the full
stature of our spirits.

"The first fruits of repentance is baptism; and baptism cometh by faith unto the fulfilling the commandments; and the fulfilling the commandments bringeth remission of sins; and the remission of sins bringeth meekness, and lowliness of heart; and because of meekness and lowliness of heart cometh the visitation of the Holy Ghost." (Moroni 8:25-26).

The blessing we receive as
we partake of the Sacrament is that
the Lord will give unto us "line upon
line, precept upon precept, here a little
and there a little; and blessed are those
who hearken unto (His) precepts, and
lend an ear unto (His) counsel, for
they shall learn wisdom; for
unto him that receiveth
(He) will give more."
(2 Nephi 28:30).

Because of
the Sacrament,
the Light of our lives
grows brighter and even
"brighter until the perfect
day." (D&C 50:24). "Trailing
clouds of glory do we come,
from God, who is our Home."
(William Wordsworth).

After we have
partaken of the Sacrament
we are easily entreated, and we
are firm in our obedience to every
one of God's commandments. But for
the conflagration of sin to be initiated,
all that is needed is combustible fuel, an
ignition temperature, and oxygen. We must
live in the world, but we don't have to be
of the world. We can't allow the heat of
the moment to get the better of us. The
Sacrament reintroduces us to the strait
and narrow way that detours us past
the ammunition dumps that are the
stockpiles of the Devil. The only
lighter we carry is that of the
Spirit, and that poses no
danger of accidental
explosion.

Every time we partake of the Sacrament, and we renew our covenant of baptism with Heavenly Father, we reaffirm that obedience is no longer inconvenient, but has become our quest. In that moment, said Ezra Taft Benson, God endows us with power. When we are diligent in our obedience, our agency enjoys its greatest expression. This is one of the hardest things for the unconverted to understand.

After the
conclusion of
our Sacrament service,
our Heavenly Father may
uses the Spirit to show us our
weaknesses, for they can become
a primer on midwifery, facilitating
the arduous process of the growth
and development of our
testimonies.

We
persevere
in our obedience
to the covenant of
the Sacrament, because
we have a strong testimony
that the principles governing
the Fall of Adam, as well as the
Savior's Atonement, were great and
eternal purposes that were prepared
from the foundation of the world.
We trace that obedience back to
our baptism itself, that testified
of our desire to participate in
every element of the Plan
of Salvation.

The Sacrament is a reminder that the poor, the unlearned, the common person, and the native born, may equally come unto Christ. Its beauty is that one size fits all. It has been designed to meet the needs of every one of Heavenly Father's children.

In
the
law,
there is
universal
applicability
that allows us
to break free of
our limiting beliefs,
which are those stories
we tell on ourselves that
sabotage our best efforts.
The Sacrament releases the
power of our potential. Its
magic is just waiting for
our wits to grow sharper
so we can be inspired
by the Holy Ghost.

One of the purposes of the Sacrament is that it catalyzes our resolve to bear testimony to the world of the things we have learned by the power of the Spirit, so that our experience can be as it was on the Day of Pentecost, when the witness of Peter and the other apostles carried the day as it penetrated the hearts of all who listened, and instilled within them the desire to inquire: "What must we do if we want to inherit eternal life?"

The Sacrament facilitates both the temporal and the spiritual implementation of The Plan. The covenant helps us to monitor our relationship with God during our engagement with mortality. The Plan is founded upon various points of doctrine that focus on salvation, and upon these elements hinges its correct understanding.

The Sacrament blesses those who are poor in spirit, and so it blesses us to "mourn with those that mourn." (Mosiah 18:9). We smile with all our heart and with all our might. If we do nothing else, we can be the smile on the faces of those who stand in need of our comfort.

The covenant of the Sacrament has been designed to make saints of sinners as it works on us to hate our former lives in the world, and to strive to be better than we have ever been before. We find compassionate ways to minister to the needs of others. We are pushed out of our comfort zones, and are nudged away from complacency and indifference, that can be suffocating to our spirits.

We receive the Sacrament so that, with the guidance of the Holy Ghost, we can become better equipped to forge relationships on earth that will be able to endure in heaven.

We take the time
during quiet moments,
as the bread and water are
passed to the congregation, to
listen for the voice of the Lord
that is unto all, for "there is none
to escape; and there is no eye that
shall not see, neither ear that shall
not hear, neither heart that shall
not be penetrated." (D&C 1:2).
We are considerate of the
feelings of others, as we
maintain the reverence
that should exist in
the Lord's holy
house.

In the
Sacrament,
the Holy Ghost,
becomes the author
of our acumen, the avatar
of our agency, the architect
of our aptitude, the benefactor of
all of our blessings, the designer of
our discipleship, the initiator of insight,
the inventor of intelligence, the patron
of perception, the provider of praise,
the sponsor of scholarship, and the
ultimate source of understanding;
as well as the craftsman of our
comfort, the guarantor of all
gifts, and the champion of
committed Christians
everywhere.

The Sacrament clothes
us in spiritual chain-mail
as protection against the fiery
darts of the adversary. Although
telestial turf is Satan's home ground,
and the quicksand of secular humanism
and other false ideologies lies ready to
suck the unwary into the underworld
of Beelzebub, no power on earth or
hell can overthrow or defeat that
which God has decreed.

The Sacrament moves us from dependency, through independency, and then, surprisingly, to the healthy and established condition of interdependency with both man and God. It gives us the tools with which we might fashion a harmony and conformity with them without sacrificing the qualities that contribute to individuality. Whisperings from the Spirit tell us that as we are, God once was, and that as He is, we may become.

As the battle
rages in our hearts,
those who have partaken
of the Sacrament live their lives
in crescendo. The deafening roar
of their righteousness commands the
attention of the angels who wield the
sword of Justice and who only await
God's command to let it fall on
an unrepentant world. Perhaps
it is only the Sacrament that
stays their hand. (For the
time being, anyway).

We
partake of
the Sacrament,
that we might be given
the tools to burst free of
our self-imposed limitations
as the powers of heaven and
earth amplify each other,
and carry us along on
the concentric waves
of the Spirit.

We receive the Sacrament in consequence of the "evils and designs which do and will exist in the hearts of conspiring men (and women) in the last days." (D&C 89:4). Angels will attend us after we have partaken. They will go before our faces, and will be on our right hand and on our left hand, and the Spirit of the Lord will be in our hearts, as heavenly angels gather around us, to bear us up. (See D&C 84:88).

When we partake of the emblems of bread and water, we are struck by the realization that when the Lord gives us commandments, He also prepares ways for us to accomplish the tasks that are set before us. We see what might be best for ourselves and for the Kingdom of God, develop a testimony that it should be, and then work with all our capacity to make it happen, whatever the cost might be. Then, when we are so richly blessed far beyond the measure that we deserve, the price, once paid so painfully, is recalled in gladness. We receive full value. As D&C 82:10 suggests: "I the Lord am bound when ye do as I say, but when ye do not what I say, ye have no promise."

The Sacrament
comes to our assistance
when we chart the unknown
possibilities of our existence.
We sweep aside the self-limiting
belief that "the sky is the limit." In
its stead, we substitute the mind
and soul expanding certainty
that "the wide expanse of
heaven is the limit."

The
Pearl
of Great
suggests that
we participate
in the Sacrament
because we desire to
become more observant
followers of righteousness,
to possess greater knowledge,
to be the progenitors of nations
and ambassadors of peace, and to
receive instruction, and keep
the commandments.

The golden cobblestones of the stairway to the stars are illuminated by the principles of true conversion. These point us in the direction of the recognition of our iniquity, and then to a deep godly sorrow for our sins. Next comes inescapable suffering and torment that stimulates an appeal to the Savior, with an awakening understanding of the Atonement. After our baptism comes the remission of our sins, spiritual enlightenment, and great joy. This motivates us to pursue a lifestyle of righteousness and service that is punctuated by our weekly observance of the Sacrament of the Lord's Supper. Each time this occurs, the endless loop cycles one more time, but, praise the God of miracles, it is calibrated each time to a higher plane of existence.

When we have the Spirit to be with us, the scriptures are "laid open to our understandings, and the true meaning and intention of their more mysterious passages (is) revealed unto us in a manner which we never could attain to previously, nor ever before had thought of." (J.S.H. 1:74).

Our Sacrament meeting is a great venue to learn the grammar of the Gospel. We approach the ordinance with confidence that "at the banquet of consequences, we will be able to bow our heads in reverence, rather than hang them in shame, in the presence of God who will be there." (Marion D. Hanks).

The arrogant, boastful, conceited, haughty, and self-centered nature of the proud is easily trumped by the altruistic, modest, deferential, and self-effacing behavior of those whose firm grasp on the Sacrament confirms their faith in the power of the Holy Ghost.

Unlike
the repentant
who approach the
Sacrament in humility,
those who are proud are
more comfortable with their
own perception of truth than
they are with God's omniscience.
They pit their own abilities against
His priesthood power, their own
paltry overtures against His
mighty works, and their
stubborn won't against
His gentle will.

All of us are repeatedly faced with occasions when withdrawals must be made from our spiritual bank accounts. When we rely upon the Sacrament, we put the principle of repentance to its ultimate test. We do not write checks that can't be cashed. We know that only after regular deposits have been made over a period of time, can we rely upon the cornucopia of comfort created by the cushion of confidence that is a currency flowing from conduct that is consistent with the core curriculum of contrition.

After we have received the Sacrament, because of the gift of the Spirit we become receptive to flashes of insight. We are cast off into streams of revelation that carry us along in the quickening currents of direct experience with our Heavenly Father, with Jesus Christ and with the Holy Ghost.

Our desire to partake of the spirit of the Sacrament fosters an atmosphere of collaboration, cooperation, and conciliation, and encourages us to share our resources with others in order to achieve solutions to their problems and find answers to their challenges that can be to our mutual advantage.

Unlike those who receive the Sacrament, the proud stubbornly hold to their own opinions rather than yielding themselves to God's direction. They fill their own lamps with oil, but are penurious when sharing their wealth with others.

It is
our honesty with
ourselves that tests the
mettle of our convictions.
With our commitment to the
Sacrament, we are putting our
money where our mouth is. We
have no proof until we act on
the basis of trust. Then, comes
the confirmation of the reality
as feelings of self-confidence
grow and purposeful actions
replace tentative overtures.
In effect, we let go
and let God.

Timid souls
who are cautiously
hesitant and tentatively
faithful don't consciously
intend to ignore the spiritual
promptings that urge them to
attend Sacrament meeting.
Desire just fades away
like the slow leak in
a bicycle tire, and
not as a sudden
blowout.

The Day of Judgment does not lie beyond a distant horizon, but begins today. We speak, think, and act according to the celestial, terrestrial, and telestial laws that are before us. Just as a barometer is used to measure the direction in which the weather is headed, so our desire to participate in Sacrament meeting helps us to be aware of the direction we must follow if we hope to regain the shelter of our heavenly home.

The Last Days mirror
the final days of Mormon, who
wrote that "there were sorceries, and
witchcrafts, and magics, and the power of
the evil one was wrought upon all the face
of the land" because of the lack of faith of
the people. (Mormon 1:19). The Sacrament
is the spiritual equivalent of enjoying a
power bar or energy drink 30
minutes before engaging
in physical activity.

The cataracts that are created by our concessions to sin cloud our vision. Our narrow perspective forces us into making comfortless compromises, leaving the landscapes of our lives as nothing more than empty shells. If we do not take advantage of the therapy of the Sacrament, the prognosis will be poor for eyes that have lost the ability to see clearly, and that can no longer make the vital distinctions between good and evil, and between light and darkness.

Perfect
faith impels
us to action. When
we follow up on our
righteous impressions,
it is as though we have
enjoyed Heavenly Father's
perfect understanding. We
eagerly look forward
to the Sacrament.

If our hearts are
hardened against the
the power of the Sacrament,
it will be as though our portion
has been diminished further. Our
natural defenses against the tactics
of the Devil will crumble, and when
we turn to face our demons and
fight our battles, we will be
terrifyingly alone.

Spiritual neglect requires drastic action. The plastic surgery of repentance, baptism, and the Sacrament is indicated if we want to experience a reversal of our fortunes, and if we ever hope to assume the likeness and the image of God in our countenances.

Our salvation has less to do with cherubim and a flaming sword, and more to do with our faith, repentance, Atonement, baptism, forgiveness, mercy, the Sacrament, and, ultimately, redemption.

The Devil was a liar
from the beginning, and
attempted to foil The Plan of
Salvation by the substitution of
his own counterfeit, unworkable
alternative that would not have
required repentance, baptism, the
Atonement, or the Sacrament.
Fortunately, in the Council
in Heaven, we were able
to see through his
deception. We
still do.

The Atonement has purpose and meaning only for those who are willing to sacrifice their broken heart and contrite spirit to the Savior of the world.

After we have partaken of the Sacrament, our lives open up in an expansion of eternal opportunities as we are personally sanctified through the receipt of the Holy Ghost. We learn what it means to have the Spirit of God to be with us.

The raw and ugly contamination of sin is incompatible with the uncompromising standard of spiritual hygiene that is required of those who have partaken of the Sacrament and hope to inhabit heaven to live in the company of God and angels.

The Sacrament is a principle that can be tested only after we have nurtured a companionship with the Holy Ghost. When we fall under His spell, however, we will be at-one with the Savior of the world.

When
we have
been born
again thru the
Sacrament, our
orientation is more
toward the expansive
laws of the eternal world
than it is to the restrictive
confines that are defined by
our physical surroundings. The
Spirit guides us to the physicality
of heartfelt repentance, and to
a spiritual appreciation of the
otherworldly doctrine of the
Atonement. God's Plan
bridges both time
and space.

The Sacrament can catalyze our relationship with God, when it unshackles us from the icy grip of our captivity to Satan. All is because of the Atonement of Christ.

Our renewal thru the Sacrament doesn't give us license to act recklessly, or to be drawn, even occasionally, to the Dark Side, or, from time to time, to be free to sample Babylon's pleasures.

Yielding to the enticements of Satan leaves us gasping for a breath of the celestial air that can only be found in the ventilation systems that service our Sacrament meetings. We go there every Sabbath day seeking respite from the choking winds that, during the week, have raked across the barren deserts of Babylon.

The
unrepentant are
argumentative; they
abuse their position and
exercise unrighteous dominion,
while those who are driven to the
Sacrament by repentance speak softly,
seek peaceful solutions to their problems,
invite the Spirit to guide them, and allow
their love of God and others to be the
engine that drives their behavior.

Those who seize the power of the Sacrament are long-suffering and they are faithful. When things seem that they could be no worse, they are at their best, because then they are especially sensitive to the comforting guidance that comes thru the whisperings of the Spirit.

Habitual sin is a quicksand that mires the unwary in a monotonously repetitive and underwhelming convention, and in a mind-numbing conformity. These are the opposites of the imaginative spontaneity and the refreshingly distinctive artistic individuality of those who enjoy the Spirit through their repetitive participation in the Sacrament.

Sometimes
all too quickly,
and sometimes agonizingly
slowly, those who have sold their
souls to the Devil for a mess of pottage
are dragged down to a hell on earth that
is of their own construction. Their bad habits
are simply the result of repetitively impulsive
behaviors that, in a rising tide of wickedness,
continually erode away at the foundations of
agency. They are fettered by the heavy chains
of compulsion. Too late, they realize that
recurring participation in the ordinance
of the Sacrament would have been a
better use of their energies, time,
and talents. It could have been
the key to their liberation
from incarceration to
sinful habits.

From
the enlightened
perspective of Mercy, the
Savior has negotiated with Justice
to purchase our sins with the legally
recognized currency of the Atonement.
His voluntary act of sacrifice is perfectly
balanced and attuned to accomplish the
task at hand, which is augmented by
faith, repentance, baptism, the Gift
of the Holy Ghost, and finally,
by the Sacrament, which is an
ordinance of renewal.

The opposite of the
path to Calvary is the road to
self-indulgence; the opposite of
our submission to the will of God
is self-gratification; the opposite of
our reverential worship during the
administration of the Sacrament
is idolatry. It is that plain
and simple.

The insolvency of Satan's seduction cannot be mitigated by third-party bailouts. The only resolution to his nepotism is for us to remember the Sacrament.

The Sacrament allows us to make mistakes, to learn from them, and to then grasp the horns of sanctuary so that at the end of the day we may still be justified by the grace of God.

Agency and opposition are always before us, and the Sacrament stands as a sacred sentinel, inviting us to enter in at heaven's gate, to find the Rest of God.

The
Devil urges
us to stay on
a detour from the
Sacrament table that
will transport us into
telestial traffic jams,
religious roundabout,
and doctrinal dead
ends, from which
escape is only
possible with
repentance.

The ordinance of the Sacrament shepherds us thru the growing pains and mental, emotional, spiritual, and physical instability that are related to early childhood development. It may only be after we have partaken of the Sacrament a few thousand times that we will have matured sufficiently in the Gospel to finally appreciate its significance.

The Sacrament, together with the Atonement of Jesus Christ, makes life eternal, love immortal, and death only a horizon, which is nothing, save the limit of our sight.

No matter that, for all intents and purposes, we have become dead weight, the Savior has the strength to carry us until we have been revitalized thru the Sacrament, and because of the powerful influence of the Holy Ghost, we once again are able to walk and not be weary, and run and not faint.

It is
nothing less
than the heavy
burden of sin that
motivates us to drag
our battered and beaten
bodies to the local chapter
of Weight Watchers, known as
Sacrament meeting of The
Church of Jesus Christ
of Latter-day
Saints.

Conduct that is sinful might look fashionable to some, but the styles that are popular today don't wear so well in our Sacrament meetings.

Our spiritual neglect requires that we take drastic action. Intensive care at the Sacrament will be necessary if we ever hope to experience a reversal of our fortunes and if, when the bandages finally come off, we expect to look in the mirror and see the likeness and image of God in our countenances.

The
Sacrament
reveals an easy way
for us to increase our
metaphysical metabolism,
to burn away as much of
the fat of faithlessness as
we can, when our hearts
are broken and melt
in the swelteringly
hot crucible of
contrition.

Our salvation has less to do with cherubim and a flaming sword, and more to do with how we deal with the Sacrament.

Because there exist no dry cleaning solvents to deal with the stain of sin, we will remain unclean in the sight of God for as long as we refuse the healing waters of baptism, and rebuff God's invitation to attend our Sacrament meetings.

Without the
steadying influence of
the Sacrament, we cannot
reasonably expect to inherit
the glory of celestial realms;
especially if we have aforetime
been agreeable to abide by only
telestial or terrestrial principles
that put fewer demands upon
our discipleship.

Faith is dead, without the accompanying work of repentance that is made possible by the Atonement and continually fortified as we partake of the Sacrament. Our faith notwithstanding, we do not have the power to save ourselves from the unalterable demands of Justice. That Mercy might abound, Heavenly Father created both our covenants and all the ordinances of the Gospel.

When we
exercise free will that
can only be carried out in
an atmosphere of opposition,
undesirable consequences are
likely to follow. Their effects
can only be mitigated by our
partaking of the Sacrament,
that follows on the heels
of repentance.

Our failure to apply the Sacrament is a form of rebellion against our Heavenly Father. As was the case following the insurgency of Lucifer, there need to be consequences, though they may be eternally damaging in their scope.

The Sacrament is a constructive process that has been designed to build us up, even if it has to first tear us down. It is involved with recovery, to be sure. But its primary focus is on discovery.

The Sacrament is witnessed by the Spirit of Justification. It asks us to consider the possibility that, one day, we might actually be holy and without spot, as is our Lord and Savior.

The raw and ugly contamination of sin is incompatible with the uncompromising standard of spiritual hygiene that is required of those who have partaken of the Sacrament, and who one day hope to inhabit heaven and live in the company of God and angels.

When we
are dealing
with weaknesses
in our contractions
that push forward the
Lord's agenda, relying on
the power of the Atonement
and considering the efficacy
of the Sacrament quickens us
to bear our solemn witness
with renewed conviction,
to the convincing of
both the Jew and
Gentile.

The Sacrament teaches us to suppress the natural inclinations of the telestial world that surround us, continually encroaching upon our spiritual stability, and threatening to erode our faith and testimony of the principles of the Gospel.

As we partake of the Sacrament, and we think of the sins for which we have repented, we will remember them only in the sense that they strengthen our testimonies and consolidate our resolve to refrain from repeating them, but we will no longer feel the guilt that was associated with the transgression.

Our progress now and in eternity hinges largely upon what do we do with the Atonement, and upon what the Sacrament does for us.

Our repentance is completed when we have partaken of the Sacrament and the Holy Ghost fills our hearts with joy. When we are clean, we enjoy a peace of conscience that defies any explanation.

About The Author

Phil Hudson and his wife Jan have 7 children and over 25 grandchildren. They enjoy spending time with their family at their cabin nestled in the Selkirk Mountains, on the shore of Priest Lake, the crown jewel of North Idaho. Phil had a successful dental practice in Spokane, Washington for 43 years, before retiring in 2015. He has an eclectic mix of hobbies, and enjoys the out of doors. He always finds time, however, to record his thoughts on his laptop, and understands Isaac Asimov's response when he was asked: If you knew that you had only 10 minutes left to live, what would you do?" He answered: "I'd type faster."

Phil received the inspiration to write this book while he and Jan were serving as missionaries for The Church of Jesus Christ of Latter-day Saints, in the Kingdom of Tonga. While there, they celebrated their 50th wedding anniversary.

We partake of the Sacrament "unto the confounding of false doctrines and laying down of contentions." (2 Nephi 3:12).

By The Author

Essays

    Volume One: Spray From The Ocean Of Thought
    Volume Two: Ripples On A Pond
    Volume Three: Serendipitous Meanderings
    Volume Four: Presents Of Mind
    Volume Five: Mental Floss
    Volume Six: Fitness Training For The Mind And Spirit

First Principles and Ordinances Series

    Faith - Our Hearts Are Changed Through Faith On His Name
    Repentance - A Broken Heart and a Contrite Spirit
    Baptism - One Hundred And One Reasons Why We Are Baptized
    The Holy Ghost - That We Might Have His Spirit To Be With Us
    The Sacrament - This Do In Remembrance Of Me

Book of Mormon Commentary

    Volume One: Born In The Wilderness
    Volume Two: Voices From The Dust
    Volume Three: Journey To Cumorah

Doctrine & Covenants Commentary

    Volume One - Sections 1 - 34
    Volume Two - Sections 35 - 57

Minute Musings: Spontaneous Combustions of Thought

    Volume One
    Volume Two
    Volume Three

Calendars:

    In His Own Words: Discovering William Tyndale
    As I Think About The Savior
    Scriptural Symbols

Children's Books

    Muddy, Muddy
    The Thirteen Articles of Faith
    Happy Birthday

Doctrinal Themes

    The House of the Lord

A Thought For Each Day Of The Year

    Faith
    Repentance
    Baptish
    The Holy Ghost
    The Sacrament
    The Temple

Professional Publications

    Diode Laser Soft Tissue Surgery Volume One
    Diode Laser Soft Tissue Surgery Volume Two
    Diode Laser Soft Tissue Surgery Volume Three

These, and other titles, are available from online retailers.

The Sacrament will always be waiting in the wings, to be applied as a balm to repair bruised egos, battered birthrights, and bitter feelings. It asks us to be brave because we are the children of God, and to be kind, because so is everyone else.

Quid magis possum dicere?

www.ingramcontent.com/pod-product-compliance
Lightning Source LLC
Chambersburg PA
CBHW060507240426
43661CB00007B/946